THE

D0221972

RILEY MOYNES

Your game plan for
Growth, Tax Relief,
and Security

Fifth
Edition

 Addison-Wesley

An imprint of Addison Wesley Longman Ltd.

ASHLAR HOUSE INC.

ISBN 0-201-31613-7

Editorial Coordination: Rosina Daillie
Design and Electronic Composition: Christine Gilham
Cover Design: Christine Gilham
Illustration & Computer Graphics: Kyle Gell, Steve MacEachern
Printing and Binding: Bryant Press

Canadian Cataloguing in Publication Data
Moynes, Riley E., 1944–
The Money Coach

Annual.
Published, 1992-1993: Copp Clark Pitman; co-published,
1995-   : Ashlar House
ISSN 1205-2728
ISBN 0-201-31613-7

1. Finance, Personal - Canada. I. Title.
HG179.M69   332.024'01'0971   C97-900999-5

Acknowledgements
Many individuals and organizations have contributed their time, support and expertise in the development of this project. Sincere thanks are extended to Jim Fraser, Lee Daugharty, Cathy Holyoke, Peter Matthews, Sabine Steinbrecher, Andy Fegarty, Peggy Adamson, Mike Connon, Albert Fong, Donna Brown, Jeff Miller, Les Petriw, Howard Back, C.A., Chris Moynes, Barry Fish and Les Kotzer, Wendy Dixon, C.A. of Equion's Advisory Services, Jennifer Jerrett, Marilyn Seguin, Al Steele of Equion's Insurance Services, Clayton Research Associates, The Fraser Institute, Loring Ward Investment Counsel, Mackenzie Financial Corporation, Canadian Institute of Actuaries, The Equion Group, Home Earnings Reverse Mortgage Corporation, the Investment Funds Institute of Canada, Royal Trust, and Vorg Incorporated.
I wish to particularly thank my wife Yvonne for her ongoing support and eternal patience; she continues to be the "wind beneath my wings."

Printed and bound in Canada

1 2 3 4 5 –BP– 01 00 99 98 97

CONTENTS

PROLOGUE

When *The Money Coach* was first published in November 1992, I had no idea how it would be received. With the exception of David Chilton's *The Wealthy Barber*, no Canadian financial book had really captured the imagination of the public at large. I was convinced that with its easy to read style and dazzling graphics in full "technicolour", it would be very different from all the others, and that was part of our intent. But how would it be received by the public?

Five years later I am gratified at the enormous, positive response I have received. The book was selected by the Book of the Month Club. Individuals and companies within the financial industry have viewed it as an ideal means of reinforcing some key concepts with their clients — and have bought the book by the hundreds and thousands. And individual Canadians, more and more interested in the whole area of investments, tax saving and retirement planning, have embraced *The Money Coach*, sometimes literally.

With each revision and expansion, I have attempted to stick to the basics, make the information as fresh and current as possible, and introduce new concepts, topics and graphics. Often, new concepts and graphics were field tested during seminars at which I am invited to speak across the country.

In 1995, I added a brand new chapter on Estate Planning. Research shows that over the next 15 years or so, one TRILLION dollars will pass from one generation to the next in Canada. It's therefore important to ensure that we structure the transfer properly from a legal and tax perspective in order that assets go to the people to whom we want them to go, with a minimum of legal obstacles and incurring as few charges as possible in both probate fees and income taxes.

The Money Coach is also becoming increasingly research driven. There is a growing body of research, part of which we are creating, indicating that there are strategies and approaches to investment which clearly work better than others. While past editions have referred to pertinent research, this edition and future ones will HIGHLIGHT it. As always, we must remember that, contrary to public opinion, knowledge itself is not power. Applied knowledge is powerful; so we must use the research to benefit from it.

In 1995, *The Money Coach* took on a new trim size - one that's perhaps a little easier to handle and one that's for convenience, identical to the companion work *Top Funds*. I hope that by doing so, you'll see the two books as complementary to one another and feel compelled to own them both, each year, forever.

In this edition, all charts and graphs have been updated to December 31, 1996 and in some cases to early 1997. This edition also incorporates the significant tax changes of the 1996 Federal Budget as well as minor changes made in the 1997 Federal Budget. I have also expanded the section on insurance and for the first time I have included reference to **universal life insurance** as an estate planning tool.

As I said in the original edition: "This book has been written to share with you the simple, commonsense ideas and principles that if acted upon will, over a period of time, create the assets that can help ensure the secure, worry-free retirement years we all dream of — but that very few of us achieve.

Read on, learn, enjoy, and act! You'll be glad you did."

Riley E. Moynes

INTRODUCTION

Are you winning the money "game"?

Do you know that you're playing the money game?

Like it or not, we are all forced to play this game from the time we begin to earn money through the rest of our lives. Taxes must be paid, bills must be paid, and loans must be paid. Money must be allocated for food, rent or mortgage, telephone, car payments, credit cards, insurance, new clothes for the kids, etc. Savings are necessary for that trip, for schooling, for retirement. The list seems endless.

How do you learn to play the money game successfully? The sad truth is that some people never do. Those who succeed often do so in a hit or miss fashion, more through good luck than good management. Some of us learn from parents or others, although most of what they learned was through sometimes bitter experience.

Unfortunately, very little formal attention is given to the topic in our schools. The attitude seems to be that it's either something that comes naturally (like walking and talking), or that it's not all that important. Both assumptions are very, very wrong!

Sometimes we turn to "professionals" for help, and they can be helpful in certain ways. Accountants have detailed knowledge of the Income Tax Act, and while that is important to the rules of the financial game, it's by no means the only part. Lawyers who specialize in tax law can be helpful in certain areas, but beyond that may have no particular financial expertise. A bank manager may be helpful when it comes to providing a needed mortgage or loan, or in telling you what the current GIC or savings account rates are, but there's a lot more to the game than that.

Then there's Revenue Canada. Again, someone there may be able to help you, although I've been given four different answers to the same tax-related question by four different RevCan employees!

And again, their expertise is limited to aspects and interpretations of the Income Tax Act. Even so, Revenue Canada is the ultimate referee in the money game.

So to whom do you turn to help you play the game effectively and successfully? You need a money coach. That's why this book was written: to help you understand the financial "big picture," and to help you develop the skills and knowledge necessary in order to compete successfully in the financial game. You're forced to play the game, so you might as well get all the help you can to play it well!

But good coaching does not come exclusively from a book. After you read this one, I urge you to find your own money coach who will continue to work with you. An effective coach will keep you up to date on the continual changes to the rules of the game. Your money coach will help you to further develop the financial skills you'll learn from this book by practising them with you and giving feedback on how well you're using them.

Some people call them financial advisors or planners, investment consultants, insurance agents, or stock brokers. I call them "money coaches." I urge you to find one with whom you're comfortable, in whom you have confidence, and who provides you with outstanding service. It can be a very satisfying, productive, and successful relationship as well as a positive learning experience.

And good luck as you play the financial game. I am confident that *The Money Coach* will help you play it successfully. You may even turn out to be a star in the game!

CHAPTER 1

t's not how much money you make that's important, it's how much you keep.

Quite simply, this book is about accumulating wealth so that you can become "financially free." To me, you are financially free when you can do what you want, where you want, when you want, and with whom you want. To some, that will enable travel and the acquisition of things; for others, it will enable charitable donations and assistance to family and friends.

Unfortunately, three major obstacles prevent us from keeping as much as we'd like — and as much as we deserve.

These three obstacles are:

- taxes
- inflation
- no plan

TAXES

In theory, taxes are imposed by governments at all levels and paid by Canadians in order to fund services that are required or desired by the people. These include such diverse services as national defence, transportation, highway construction, mail delivery, garbage pick up, and many others.

Unfortunately, for a variety of reasons including government mismanagement, Canadians are now among the most heavily taxed people in the world. One research group, The Fraser Institute in Vancouver, calculates that while in 1961 only 34% of the income of the average Canadian home was paid in taxes of all kinds, the figure had increased to 46% in 1996.

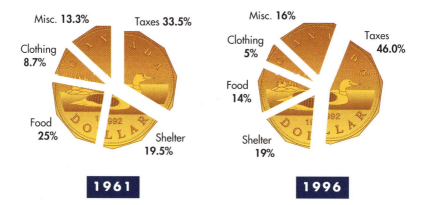

Misc. **13.3%** Taxes **33.5%**
Clothing **8.7%**
Food **25%**
Shelter **19.5%**

1961

Misc. **16%** Taxes **46.0%**
Clothing **5%**
Food **14%**
Shelter **19%**

1996

The trend appears to be inevitable: an ever increasing amount of personal income consumed by taxes.

Unfortunately, most Canadians seem to be resigned to this sorry situation. You'll learn by reading on, however, that there are several ways of reducing your tax burden and keeping more of your own money.

Think of paying taxes as a game. You probably wouldn't decide to play a game before you knew the rules — you'd be afraid of embarrassing yourself publicly, and you know that you can't play any game effectively without knowing the rules that apply. Your coach or someone teaches you the rules, and you can then play more effectively.

It's the same with taxes except that we are all forced to play the tax game — we have no choice. All the rules apply, but we don't know them well. Therefore, we play the tax game poorly. And when was the last time your friendly Revenue Canada representative called to suggest tax reduction strategies or to clarify the tax rules for you? Revenue Canada is not the coach — it's the umpire. You must either get a money coach (a financial advisor, a tax lawyer, an accountant, a trusted friend) or teach yourself. Most of us do neither. Small wonder we don't play the tax game well and therefore, pay more in taxes than is necessary!

TAX FREEDOM DAY

Tax Freedom Day is the day on which the average Canadian has earned enough to pay all local, provincial, and federal taxes.

JULY

	1	2	3	4		
5	6	7	(8)	9	10	11
12	13	14	15	16	17	18
19	20	21	22	23	24	25
26	27	28	29	30	31	

1985	**July 20**
1994	**July 22**
1996	**July 8**

Source: The Fraser Institute

This date includes government deficits, since at some point taxes will have to be higher by the amount of the deficit. Tax freedom day, excluding deficits, was June 17, 1996; it was May 3rd in 1961.

INFLATION

While most people seem to be aware of taxes (though they may not know what to do about them), they seem to be unaware of the insidiousness of inflation. It truly is a silent, stalking enemy that assaults — and can even destroy — our financial health in the same way that cancer attacks and can ruin our physical health.

In simple terms, inflation eats into and reduces our buying power on an ongoing basis. Twenty years ago, it cost 12¢ to mail a first class letter in Canada; in 1997 it costs 48¢ (45 + 3 GST)! That's inflation! If this rate of inflation continues for the next twenty years, it will cost $1.92 to mail a first class letter.

Inflation also devastates your investment returns. Over the last decade, inflation has virtually swallowed

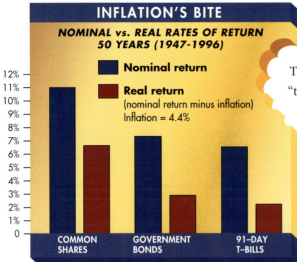

INFLATION'S BITE
NOMINAL vs. REAL RATES OF RETURN 50 YEARS (1947-1996)

Nominal return

Real return
(nominal return minus inflation)
Inflation = 4.4%

12%
11%
10%
9%
8%
7%
6%
5%
4%
3%
2%
1%
0

COMMON SHARES | GOVERNMENT BONDS | 91–DAY T–BILLS

Source: Harry H. Panjer and Keith P. Sharp,
"Report on Canadian Economic Statistics, 1924–1992,"
Canadian Institute of Actuaries, June 1996

up or offset most wage increases that have been achieved by Canadians.

The result — most people are "treading water" at best, and not getting ahead in real terms.

Inflation also hits hard at pensioners who do not have inflation protection as part of their plan. It cuts the purchasing power of a $40,000 pension in half to $20,000 in about 12 years (at an average inflation rate of 6%).

On the bright side, there is one good thing that can be said of inflation: It has allowed virtually every Canadian homeowner to live in a more expensive neighbourhood without moving.

Money Coach Rule

Always take inflation into account when calculating investment gains. It's the only way to get a true sense of the progress that has been achieved.

NO PLAN

If you don't know where you are going, any road will do. (Chinese proverb)

Unfortunately, this quotation is true for the vast majority of Canadians. Over 90% of us do nothing that could reasonably be called financial planning.

It's not that people plan to fail. Rather, they fail to plan.

Financial planning is essentially the proper handling of income and cash to meet your goals. A financial plan should be "one page simple" and generally should not include a monthly or weekly budget. I don't know anyone who became wealthy by budgeting; not only are those who try it usually unsuccessful, but they also tend to be boring conversationalists. Concentrate instead on the "big picture."

So far we have outlined the situation that many people find themselves in.

- They're paying large amounts in tax; likely more than necessary.

- They're being hurt by inflation without even realizing it.

- They don't know what they're trying to achieve and have no plan to achieve it.

Now let's look at what can and should be.

• COACH'S PLAYBOOK •

How to build a financial plan

A financial plan should contain three simple parts:

Part 1. A snapshot of where you are financially, i.e., a statement of assets, obligations, and income.

Part 2. A statement or at least a sense of where you want to be in the short term (one year) and the longer term (three to five years), i.e., a goal or goals.

Part 3. A list of actions to be taken to get you from where you are to where you want to be.

Most people have no difficulty with Parts 1 or 2 of their financial plan; Part 3 can be more difficult unless you know some of the strategies. That's what this book will help you to learn. But you should also have some help from someone you trust in putting together a series of actions to be taken or decisions to be made; in other words, find yourself a money coach.

Ideally you won't depend too much on others to help you develop and implement your plan. Ultimately, we must all take responsibility for our own financial future. Fortunately, the basic principles to help you do that are really very simple. Not only can you learn them but you can also learn to apply them. That's where the fun and the results come!

HERE'S WHAT A SIMPLE FINANCIAL PLAN LOOKS LIKE:

PART 1

GENERAL INFORMATION

YES	NO	
○	○	1. Do you have a current will?
○	○	2. Do you have a child/grandchild education fund?
○	○	3. Do you anticipate a significant inheritance?
○	○	4. Do you face any major life changes (marriage, job, move)?
○	○	5. Is your home registered jointly with your spouse?

6. What is your current income from all sources?

_____

7. What is the approximate rate of return on your current RRSP?

_____

8. How much life insurance coverage do you have?

_____

9. How much income tax did you pay last year?

_____

10. How many years to expected retirement?

_____

11. Expected retirement income?

_____

CURRENT NET WORTH

ASSETS

Savings _____

Stocks, bonds, mutual funds _____

Home _____

Other property _____

Autos _____

RRSP's _____

Other _____

Total assets _____

OBLIGATIONS

Mortgage PIT _____

Credit cards _____

Loans _____

Support payments _____

Line of credit _____

Other mortgages _____

Other _____

Total obligations _____

Net Worth _____
(assets-obligations)

ASSESSMENT

What aspects of your current situation are you:

Most pleased about?

_____
_____
_____
_____
_____

Least pleased about?

_____
_____
_____
_____
_____
_____

PART 2

What are your current financial priorities? (e.g., buy new car, pay off mortgage, pay less tax, save for vacation, renovate, etc.)

_____
_____
_____
_____
_____

Where do you want to be financially in 5 to 10 years? (e.g., have no mortgage, pay less tax, acquire an investment portfolio, prepare for retirement, start your own business.)

_____
_____
_____
_____
_____
_____

THE THREE GOALS OF FINANCIAL INDEPENDENCE

I'm convinced that if people patiently and consistently focus on the following simple financial goals, they would be well on the road to financial independence.

These goals will represent different priorities for different people depending on their age and circumstances. But taken together, they represent a very powerful set of objectives.

We can achieve all three key objectives. But to do so, we must be prepared to make some decisions that do not always have "guaranteed" results. I'm convinced this is the preferred way to go.

These few pages have attempted to set the stage for later chapters and to put the more specific suggestions that follow in perspective.

We have identified your financial goals of growth, tax relief, and security. You know, at least in general terms, where you want to go. You're ready to examine the strategies and suggestions that lie ahead. You're ready to put your game plan into effect.

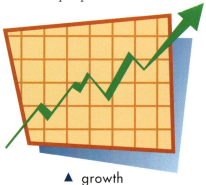

▲ growth

◀ tax relief

▼ security

CHAPTER 2

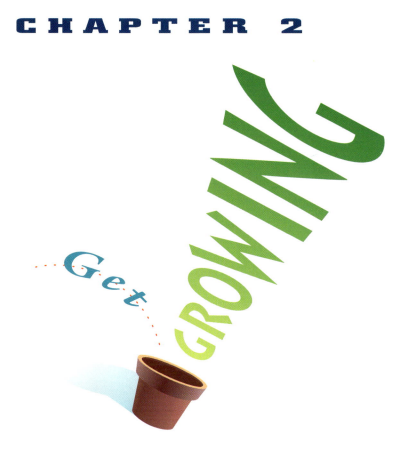

A strong commitment to seek growth is vital for two main reasons:

1. To avoid being limited exclusively to pension income in retirement

ome Canadians are fortunate because they belong to a pension plan where they work. But even the best of these plans will provide only up to a maximum of 70% of your pre-retirement income in retirement. Many Canadians will live in retirement on as little as 25% of their former income, and that prospect is scary.

Fewer than one half of all Canadians are enrolled in a Registered Retirement Savings Plan (RRSP) or company pension plan, and one third have no savings or investment program for retirement.

INCOME GAP AT RETIREMENT

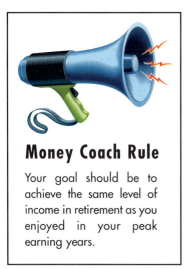

$50,000 –
$40,000 –
$30,000 –
$20,000 –
$10,000 –
0 –

Pre-Retirement
Income

Canada Pension Plan
& Old Age Security
after retirement

At most, benefits from the Canada Pension Plan and Old Age Security replace only about one quarter of your earnings. The maximum currently available from all government sources is a little more than $1,100 per month, and there are growing concerns about the future viability of the government's retirement security system as our population continues to age and fewer younger people contribute to it.

Contributions to CPP are projected to rise substantially over the next several decades, and if future generations of voters ultimately reject higher contributions as politically unacceptable, governments will be forced to dramatically reduce the plan's payouts. As a result, Canadians will have to fall back more and more on their own resources in retirement.

Money Coach Rule

Your goal should be to achieve the same level of income in retirement as you enjoyed in your peak earning years.

Some people seem to think that's okay, and they'll simply adjust their retirement life-style accordingly. I say you shouldn't be prepared to accept anything less in retirement than the income you enjoyed in your peak earning years!

After all, you'll have more time available (about one quarter to one third of your life). You've spent your whole life working and often putting off doing things you really wanted to do, like travelling. In retirement you'll have the time, but will you have the money?

Probably not if you don't do something to supplement your income. For most people, that means achieving growth in their investments before retirement. We'll offer specific suggestions how starting on page 20.

Then there are those who don't have a pension at all. It's absolutely vital that these folks put money away now so they'll have a decent income when they retire and not be reliant on government cheques for support.

2. *To beat inflation and taxes by the widest margin possible*

As we noted in the previous chapter, inflation and taxes are two major adversaries as we try to get ahead financially.

Your real rate of return is what you make after taxes and inflation.

It is generally agreed that a 3% *real rate of return* is pretty good; of course, the higher the better.

The problem is that many people are simply treading water.

If you put your money in a savings account or buy term deposits, Canada Savings Bonds (CSB), or Guaranteed Investment Certificates (GICs), you're probably not getting ahead financially.

Here's why:

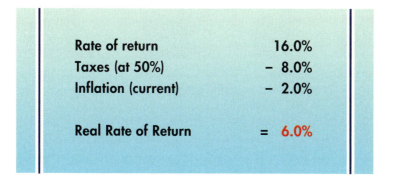

CANADA SAVINGS BONDS

Advertised Rate of Return	6.50%
Taxes (at 50%)	– 3.25%
Inflation (current)	– 2.00%
Real Rate of Return	**= 1.25%**

So, if seeking significant growth is your objective (as it should be), you will usually not achieve it by putting your money in the bank or by buying CSBs or GICs.

Wouldn't you rather experience this?

Rate of return	16.0%
Taxes (at 50%)	– 8.0%
Inflation (current)	– 2.0%
Real Rate of Return	**= 6.0%**

Now you're making progress. You achieved 16.0% return on investment, rather than settling for 6.5%, and your real rate of return is above that magic 3.0% level. It's a gain of 6.0% rather than 1.25%.

And it's easy to do. Begin building your strategy using the following steps to achieve growth.

1. START NOW!

Why start now? It's important to start now because time is a critical element in achieving growth; the earlier the better and better late than never.

Let's assume you set a goal to have $100,000 at age 65 to supplement your other sources of income at that time. Believe it or not, if you are 25 now, you can achieve this goal by saving only $10.22 per month (at 12%). Most people can find $10.22 a month if they want to, especially if they know what it will turn into at age 65.

THE $100,000 QUESTION

How much you'd have to save every month to end up with $100,000 when you reach 65

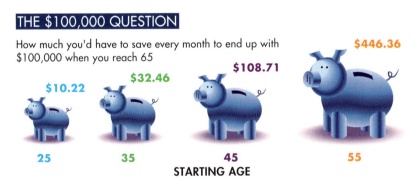

$10.22	$32.46	$108.71	$446.36
25	35	45	55

STARTING AGE

But if you're 55 now and want to achieve the same goal — $100,000 at age 65 — you're going to have to put aside $446.36 per month (at 12%) — 43 times more than you would have had to save monthly at age 25!

So it's easy to see that if you want to be financially independent, you must start now. The longer you wait, the more it will cost you to achieve your goal, as shown below.

By waiting five years before starting to invest (from age 25 to 30), it actually costs you $179,658!

THE PRICE OF WAITING

Begin savings at	Total at age 65	Cost to wait
age 25	$296,516	
age 26	$264,402	$32,114
age 30	$116,858	$179,658

$1 per day invested at 12% compounded annually to age 65

2. PAY YOURSELF FIRST: USE THE 10% SOLUTION!

At the first of each month, before you pay a single bill, write yourself a cheque for at least 10% of your income and make it part of your regular investment program.

Who deserves it more than you do? After all, you earned it.

Why is it so vital to pay yourself first?

The discouraging truth is that according to Statistics Canada, a full 43% of those over 65 must now rely on the Guaranteed Income Supplement to see them through their retirement years. They live at subsistence levels, and as can be seen from the charts on page 22, the situation is substantially worse for women.

Many are also relying on Canada Pension Plan (CPP) benefits to assist them in their old age. First of all, these benefits will not enable most people to live at the level they did during their working career and secondly, there are fewer and fewer people contributing to CPP in relation to the number drawing from it as time goes on and as the population ages.

It is quite possible that when you retire, CPP will not provide much of anything for your retirement. Canada will experience a dramatic increase in the number of seniors in the future. As a result there is no guarantee that social programs once considered universal will be continued. There is no contract with the government; programs can be wiped out.

CURRENT CANADIAN RETIREMENT SITUATION

(for those 65+)

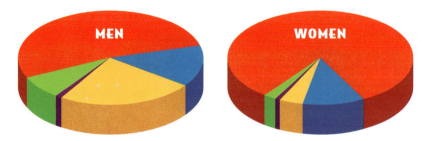

For every 100 men and women:

🔴 53 men, 82 women require financial assistance from family, friends and/or the government

🔵 14 men, 11 women are working whether they want to or not

🟢 8 men, 2 women are financially secure enjoying a lifestyle close to what they were used to when they worked

🟡 24 men, 4 women have passed away

🟣 1 man, 1 woman are wealthy

Source: Statistics Canada

Even if you contribute to a pension plan at work (and only about 40% of Canadians do), your pension income will generally not provide you with more than 60% to 70% of your peak earning income. If you don't

THE RULE OF 72

Want to know how long it will take to double your money? Just divide 72 by your investment rate of return. For example, if a mutual fund you're investing in produces an average annual compound rate of return of 12%, you will double your money in 72÷12=6 years.

Rate of Return	Time Required to Double Investment
4%	18 years
5%	14.4 years
6%	12 years
7%	10.3 years
8%	9 years
9%	8 years
10%	7.2 years
11%	6.5 years
12%	6 years

contribute to a pension plan, government assistance will provide only about 25% of your earnings in your peak earning years. The maximum one can currently receive from both Canada and provincial government plans is a little over $13,000 per year; most people receive less. And what you do receive is taxed!

Remember the goal: to retire at an income level the same as you achieved during your peak earning years. It is unwise to rely on someone else to provide for your financial future. No one cares about your future the way you do.

Money Coach Rule

Start now to supplement your pension income or to create your own pension through an investment program consisting of at least 10% of your earnings. Pay yourself first!

3. BE CONSISTENT!

Time, as we have just seen, is one key element in achieving growth.

The other significant part of the equation is consistency — but it doesn't take much money to get started, and a little will turn into a lot.

The following chart illustrates how it works. Let's assume you can invest only $120 per month over a long term and that you can obtain a 18.0% return on your money. In 25 years it'll grow to over $540,000; in 35 years, to more than $2.86 million. And in 40 years, you'll have more than $6.5 million!

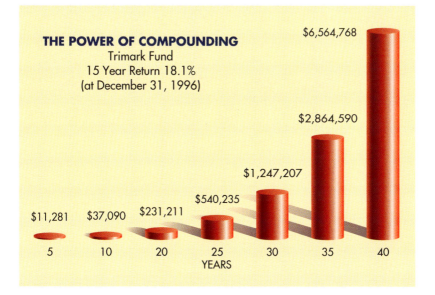

THE POWER OF COMPOUNDING
Trimark Fund
15 Year Return 18.1%
(at December 31, 1996)

$6,564,768

$2,864,590

$1,247,207

$540,235

$231,211

$37,090

$11,281

| 5 | 10 | 20 | 25 | 30 | 35 | 40 |
YEARS

Coach's Quote

"I don't know what the Seven Wonders of the World are, but I know what the Eighth Wonder is: compounding."

Baron Rothschild

It sounds unbelievable, but it's true. Time and consistency are powerful! Your $120 per month (only about $28 per week) turns into $6.5 million after 40 years.

The growth of money over time is called "compounding." And it's one of the most amazing and exciting financial concepts of all.

Many people don't think a few extra percentage points of return amount to much money. They are wrong.

Just a few percentage points of return compounded over several years can make a difference of thousands and thousands of additional dollars. Here's how it works.

The accompanying chart shows what happens when you invest $3,500 each year for 30 years at different rates:

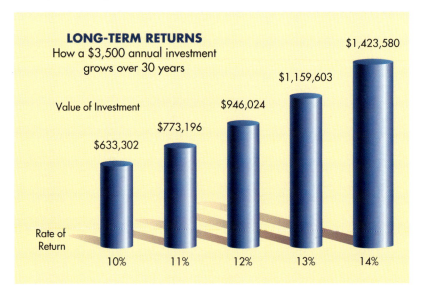

LONG-TERM RETURNS
How a $3,500 annual investment grows over 30 years

Value of Investment

$633,302
$773,196
$946,024
$1,159,603
$1,423,580

Rate of Return

10%   11%   12%   13%   14%

It's clear that the rate of return has a huge impact on the final amount of money available and reinforces the fact that we should always seek out these few extra percentage points of return, in order to achieve the greatest growth possible.

Note that a difference of only 1% (from 10% to 11%) produces an added return of about $140,000.

• COACH'S PLAYBOOK •

Pay off your bank loans and credit cards

It's true that debt — a bank loan or a mortgage — can help to focus your attention and ensure that the payments are made. It's a form of "forced savings." Many of us won't save $100 a month but will pay back a loan at $100 a month. The effect is similar. However, there is a major difference. When you have a loan, you're paying interest on that loan! That means it's costing you money — and it's after-tax dollars.

And that is particularly true of credit cards. Several major Canadian credit cards charge interest in the range of 15% to 18%, and some rates have been higher than that. Yet, thousands of people continue to hold CSBs or GICs, which are fully taxable, at the same time that they have outstanding consumer loans. No! No! No!

One more thought. If you've got more than one loan, first pay off the one that's costing you the most. If you've got a loan at 10% and one at 8%, pay off or at least reduce the 10% loan first.

Alternatively, consider consolidating two or more outstanding loans; you may be able to negotiate a lower rate than you're paying now and you may be able to reduce your monthly payments at the same time. In short, get rid of your non-deductible debt as soon as you can. It'll make you feel great, and it's one of the best moves you can make!

Money Coach Rule

Pay Yourself 10% First + Start Early + Magic of Compounding = Financial Independence

Money Coach Rule

The message should be clear: pay off car loans, furniture loans, travel loans, etc., and credit card balances as soon as possible! You'll be much better positioned to ensure that you can continue to use the magic 10% solution.

4. BE AN "OWNER" — NOT A "LOANER"

I can hear you now: "OK Coach," you're saying, "I'll start now; I'll invest regularly, saving 10% of my salary; I'll take advantage of the magic of compounding, and I'll make the Rule of 72 work for me. But tell me Coach, how do I get a 15% to 18% return on my money so that it doubles in four to five years?"

Achieving higher rates of return over the long term is simple. The trick is to be an *owner*, not a *loaner*.

BE AN OWNER, NOT A LOANER

Think about it: you invest $10, 000 in a 5-year G.I.C. at a guaranteed 6% in your local bank:

You earn for the year	$ 600
But... you pay taxes (at 45%) on that interest	− 270
So... your net earnings are	330
But... inflation averages 5%	− 500
Look again! You have actually suffered a loss in purchasing power of...	$ −170

What you have been "guaranteed" by the bank is a loss of purchasing power because the guaranteed interest rate can't keep up with inflation and taxes!!

What's the difference? When you're a loaner, you lend money to the government (when you buy CSBs) or to the banks (if you put money there in term deposits or in Guaranteed Investment Certificates). You receive a guaranteed rate of return, have the knowledge that your money is secure, and sacrifice substantial growth potential.

But what are you really achieving? Despite the fact that many deposits in a bank or trust company are guaranteed at a fixed rate and by Canada Deposit Insurance Corporation against loss, you may still be losing — and losing something equally important —purchasing power.

If it were consistently more advantageous for individuals and businesses to put their money in the bank than to invest in profit-seeking businesses, we would have a major problem. But that's not the case. In fact, just the opposite is true.

Despite all our complaints and the constant focus in the media on problems, we're better off than ever before. Those of us lucky enough to live in Canada, which according to a recent United Nations study is the best country in the world in which to reside, are better off than 90% of the world's population.

What's more, the next several decades will bring greater opportunities for growth than ever before in the history of humankind! The way to participate in all of this is to be an owner, not a loaner.

We know now that if you're a typical loaner, you're putting your money in the bank, or purchasing term deposits, GICs, or CSBs. But what's an owner?

An owner actually invests in the growth of the economy of this country or in the growth of the economy of other countries. While many people associate investment as an owner with investment in the stock market, this is not necessarily the case. It may involve ownership in mutual funds, real estate, or the stock market. The key is that traditionally, if your investment goes into ownership vehicles (stocks, mutual funds, real estate), your annual return may be 12% to 16% or even more. Take a look for example at the accompanying chart (TSE Trends, 1957–1997), showing the long-term growth of the stocks making up the Toronto Stock Exchange 300 Index.

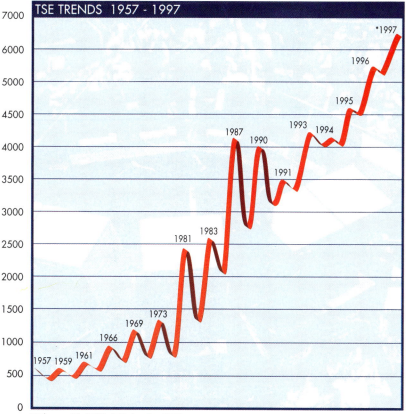

TSE TRENDS 1957 - 1997

* February 28, 1997 - TSE closed at 6158

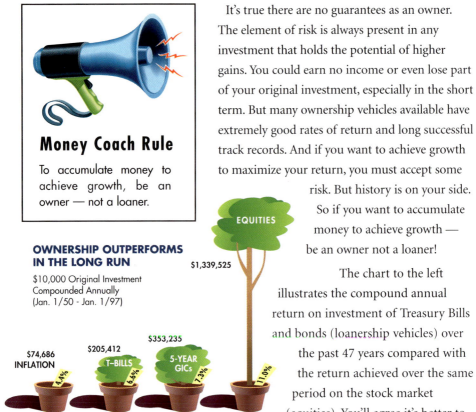

Money Coach Rule

To accumulate money to achieve growth, be an owner — not a loaner.

It's true there are no guarantees as an owner. The element of risk is always present in any investment that holds the potential of higher gains. You could earn no income or even lose part of your original investment, especially in the short term. But many ownership vehicles available have extremely good rates of return and long successful track records. And if you want to achieve growth to maximize your return, you must accept some risk. But history is on your side. So if you want to accumulate money to achieve growth — be an owner not a loaner!

The chart to the left illustrates the compound annual return on investment of Treasury Bills and bonds (loanership vehicles) over the past 47 years compared with the return achieved over the same period on the stock market (equities). You'll agree it's better to be an owner than a loaner.

OWNERSHIP OUTPERFORMS IN THE LONG RUN

$10,000 Original Investment
Compounded Annually
(Jan. 1/50 - Jan. 1/97)

EQUITIES
$1,339,525

$353,235
5-YEAR GICs
7.3%

$205,412
T-BILLS
6.6%

$74,686
INFLATION
4.4%

11.0%

Source: James Hatch and Robert White, *Canadian Stocks, Bonds, and Inflation: 1950–1987*; updated with information supplied by Scotia McLeod, Mackenzie Financial Corporation, and Andex Chart.

This chart shows how a high performance mutual fund like the Industrial Growth Fund has outperformed a variety of investments over the past 29 years.

Period from Dec. 31, 1967 to December 31, 1996.
Sources: Statistics Canada; Scotia McLeod; Toronto Stock Exchange; Bank of Canada Review; Mackenzie Financial Corporation.

INDUSTRIAL GROWTH FUND: 29-YEAR GROWTH OF $50,000 – A COMPARISON

$2,411,630

Real Growth

Growth Needed to Match Inflation ($243,416)

Original Capital ($50,000)

$953,347 $912,285 $885,443 $693,471 $295,093 $243,416

| Industrial Growth Fund | TSE Total Return | Mortgages | Long-Term Bonds | 5-year GIC's | Savings Account | Inflation |

5. PUT YOUR MONEY TO WORK IN MUTUAL FUNDS

WHAT IS A MUTUAL FUND?

A mutual fund is a "pool" of money to which thousands of people contribute. This pool of money is managed by professional money managers who invest the money in Treasury Bills (T-Bills), safe and secure government or corporate bonds, and in shares of generally proven Canadian and international corporations. They keep a watchful eye on the economy, on political, demographic and economic trends, and on international events in order to determine where and how the pool of money can be invested to produce the most solid long-term growth.

Coach's Quote

"When you put your money in the bank, it goes to sleep. When you put your money in a mutual fund, it goes to work!"

HOW A MUTUAL FUND WORKS

POOLED MONEY

PROFESSIONAL MANAGERS MAKE INVESTMENT DECISIONS

STOCKS   BONDS   T-BILLS   REAL ESTATE

GROWTH OF INVESTMENT

THE BENEFITS OF MUTUAL FUNDS

Professional money management

Most people are too busy to take time to effectively oversee their financial affairs. They are also not trained to be expert money managers. By buying mutual funds, these people are receiving the benefit of the experience and skills of some of the best money managers in the world whose goal is to achieve long-term growth for the money they invest.

One of the most successful mutual funds ever, the Templeton Growth Fund, which is managed by John Templeton and his management team, is a good example. Those who invested $10,000 in this fund when it began in 1954 saw their investment grow to be worth over $4.1 million by January 31, 1997. That's an average annual compounded growth rate of 15.5%!

Canada's Trimark Fund was launched in 1981. A $10,000 investment at the time grew to $127,050 by December 31, 1996. The average annual compound rate of return to December 31, 1996 was 15.4% over ten years and 18.0% since inception. The fund is managed by the Trimark Investment Management Inc. which manages more than $21 billion for over 1,000,000 investors.

Diversification

Most people aren't wealthy enough to be able to diversify properly on their own by buying stocks of various companies in a number of countries. Because of the size of the mutual fund "pool," often totalling millions or billions of dollars, investors can purchase a share of a vast array of securities, bonds, and other investments. This allows you to achieve the peace of mind that comes from "not putting all your eggs in one basket."

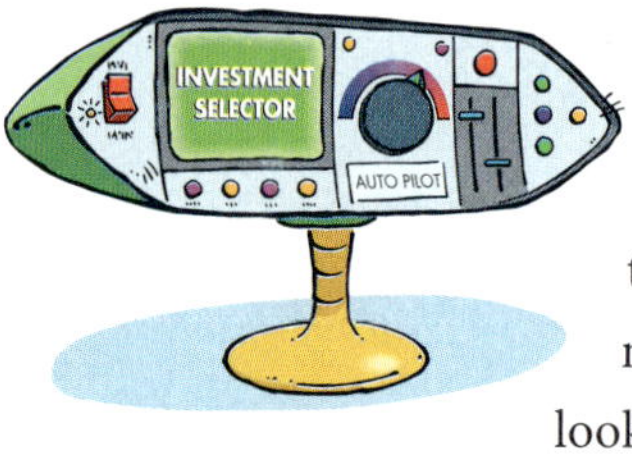

"Hands-off" investment

As mentioned earlier, most people don't have the time, inclination, or expertise to do the research necessary to make wise investment decisions. This is all looked after for investors by professional money managers for whom this is a full-time job.

Lots of choice

Regardless of your circumstances, there are mutual
funds that can meet your needs. Some people want
income now; others, who will require income later,
opt for growth now. Some investors are aggressive,
while others are much more conservative. Some
select equity funds, others prefer real estate funds,
and still others like mortgage funds — or a
mixture of each. Some wish to invest in specialty funds
like gold; others like to invest in specific foreign regions like Japan or
Europe. With several hundred funds available to select from, there is truly
a fund to meet virtually every need.

In addition to these major benefits, there are other attractive features,
too:

● Most funds allow initial purchases as low as $50 to $100.

● Most funds make it very easy to invest with a lump sum, pre-authorized
  chequing on a regular basis or through a group purchase with automatic
  payroll deduction.

● Mutual funds are "liquid" and can be sold easily and quickly; there is no
  minimum length of time required to hold the funds.

● Many funds are structured so that there is no acquisition fee and,
  depending on how long you hold the fund, there may be no exit fee either.

● A systematic withdrawal plan that meets your individual needs can be
  established as you near retirement and may require regular income.

It is important to note that mutual funds should be seen as long-term
investments (i.e., they should be held for at least five years). Over this
extended period of time, the economy and the market will most likely
continue to develop and grow as will the value of your investments. For those
willing and able to hold their shares over the long term, there will be little
need for concern. But for those who might consider purchasing for a hold of
only a year or two, there is a greater degree of risk and the value of their
funds might actually end up being lower than when they were purchased. For
that reason, it's best to view a mutual fund as a long-term investment. When
you do that, you have history on your side, for over the long term, mutual
funds (which represent *ownership*) have significantly outperformed GICs
(which represent *loanership*).

What accounts for the extraordinary growth of mutual funds in the past
decade? Much of it, I believe, can be attributed to an increasingly complex

world which is changing so fast that individual investors are no longer able to function comfortably. The result has been a dramatic move in Canada and worldwide to "managed money."

For most people, this has been through mutual fund investments, although other managed-money vehicles have also emerged — including closed-end funds, wrap accounts, REITs (real estate investment trusts), "investment" life insurance, limited partnerships, and private money management.

The trend towards managed money — although certainly helped by low interest rates and generally positive market conditions — has been driven largely by the growing number of people who recognize that they are no longer restricted to the traditional choice of Guaranteed Investment Certificates (GICs), Canada Savings Bonds (CSBs), Treasury Bills or term deposits on one hand, and direct stock market investment on the other. It's based as well on an understanding that an extra single-percentage-point return, when compounded over the long term, can yield significantly more accumulated wealth; and it's based on a belief that a full-time professional will almost always achieve better investment results than a part-time amateur.

All of these events have contributed to phenomenal growth in the mutual fund industry in Canada, as shown below:

FUND PHENOMENON

Actual and projected growth of the Canadian mutual fund industry

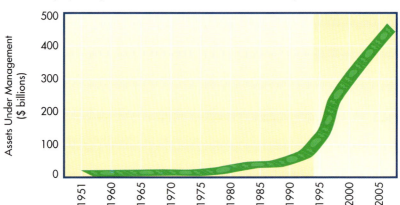

And the growth shows no sign of slowing down. In fact, a report prepared by Gordon Capital Corp. in September 1993 predicts that assets under management by the Canadian mutual fund industry will soar to $474 billion by the end of 2002. At the time of writing, they are about $232 billion.

• TYPES OF MUTUAL FUNDS •

1. Money Market Funds

Money Market Funds invest in short term money market instruments such as Treasury Bills whose maturities are less than one year. The objective is to provide a better return than savings accounts with minimal risk of capital. Money market instruments are very safe and have the highest available credit ratings among securities. These funds offer safety and liquidity.

2. Income or Mortgage Funds

These funds invest primarily in mortgages, as well as in other fixed income securities, such as bonds, and mortgage backed securities. The objective is to provide attractive income returns versus other fixed income securities (i.e., term deposits, GICs, etc.), with a high degree of safety.

3. Bond Funds

Bond funds primarily invest in government and corporate bonds and debentures, but many hold other fixed income securities. The objective is to provide income as well as safety afforded by government and corporate debt securities. Bond funds have moderate growth potential, especially when interest rates decline.

4. Balanced Funds

Balanced funds invest in a cross section of securities including bonds, debentures, preferred shares, common shares, and cash. The objective is to provide a combination of safety (stability) through fixed income investments and dividend paying stocks and growth through common shares.

5. Dividend Funds

Dividend funds invest in a diversified portfolio of preferred shares and some common shares. Dividends from taxable

Canadian corporations are subject to reduced taxes through the dividend tax credit. The objective is to provide attractive income returns on an after tax basis to investors. These funds also offer moderate growth potential.

6. Real Estate Funds

Real Estate funds invest in a diversified portfolio of real estate holdings. The objective is to provide attractive income as well as growth potential through the appreciation potential of the real estate holdings.

7. Equity Funds (also referred to as Common Stock Funds or Growth Funds)

Equity funds invest primarily in common shares of corporations. The equity funds available range from the very conservative blue chip funds to speculative or venture funds. Equity funds vary in the level of diversification and risk involved, but most funds have growth as their major investment objective. Some funds also generate dividend income. Historically returns on common shares have outperformed fixed income securities. However, on a year-to-year basis, common share returns can be volatile.

THE BEST WAYS TO INVEST IN MUTUAL FUNDS

Depending on your investment style, your level of expertise, and the amount of time you feel you can afford to devote to managing your portfolio personally, several investment strategies may be of interest and of help.

THE "DOLLAR COST AVERAGING" STRATEGY

This is probably the best and simplest way for people to invest in mutual funds.

Ideally, every investor seeks to buy at a low price and sell at a higher price at a later date. The question is how to do that, given the fact that there are market fluctuations. Nobody seems to mind the upward trends; it's those slides that upset us so much. However, by using a simple strategy called "dollar cost averaging", even the downside fluctuations can actually work to your advantage! It's as close as one can get to infallible investing — and most people don't even know about it.

Psychologically, if you are committed to regular investments and if you are prepared to invest over the long term, then downward trends (which are bound to come along) are simply opportunities to buy additional shares at lower-than-usual prices. As always, of course, the upward trends will continue to be rewarding and satisfying.

Let's see how it actually works by using the following three examples. We're going to invest $100 a month for nine years (i.e., $12,000 will be invested).

SCENARIO 1

Because the unit prices constantly increase, the number of units purchased each year actually declines as the chart shows. For example, in year one, the unit price is $6.00 and therefore $1,200 per

year ($100 per month) buys 200 units. By the end of year six, the unit price has increased to $8.50, and therefore $1,200 buys only 141 units. At the end of nine years, when the unit price is $10, the value of the portfolio is $13,869 — a 28% increase.

SCENARIO 2

Notice here that for the first five years, the unit price declines. Imagine how happy you'd be in that situation! But patience is rewarded. The result of lower unit prices is that a larger number of units

Money Coach Rule

Use dollar cost averaging as an effective system for buying mutual funds (or stocks) on a regular basis (usually monthly) with a fixed amount of money (usually $100 – $300).

are purchased while you continue to invest $100 per month. Note that in Scenario 2 the original purchase price and the final purchase price are the same ($6). There is no market rise at all.

Despite this, 2,150 units have been acquired in this scenario. And even at a $6 unit price at the end of nine years, the value of the portfolio is $12,898 — a 19% increase. Significant growth in the value of your investment actually occurs in a declining and recovering market. You get the benefit of purchasing more mutual fund units when prices are at a reduced value.

SCENARIO 3

Here the unit price increases and decreases over time. Therefore, more units are purchased with the $1,200 in some years than in others. This example is probably the most realistic in reflecting actual conditions. After nine years, the number of units purchased is greater than in Scenario 1 — 1,479 to be exact. At $10 per unit at the end of year nine, the investment is worth $14,787 — a 37% increase in value.

Thus you can see that the psychological barrier of purchasing more shares when prices are low (and that's the very best time to buy) is overcome by using dollar cost averaging. In fact, dollar cost averaging removes the problem of timing from investment management. By investing regularly, we don't get hung up on timing, for we've now got a logical comprehensive investment strategy based on confidence in the long-term health of the Canadian and international economies.

For most people, dollar cost averaging is the best way to invest.

SCENARIO #3
Averaging in a Fluctuating Market

Year	Unit Price	Units Bought
1	$6.00	200
2	$5.50	218
3	$7.00	171
4	$6.50	185
5	$8.00	150
6	$7.50	160
7	$9.00	133
8	$8.50	141
9	$10.00	120

YEARS

Units purchased = 1,479
Total cost = $10,800

Market value = $14,787
$ Growth = $3,987
% Growth = 37%

• COACH'S PLAYBOOK •

The "Best" Time to Invest

How can you predict the "BEST" vs. the "WORST" time to invest? In some cases it just may not matter!

The illustrations below cover the last 25 years and the "BEST/WORST" days on which to have invested twenty-five different $5,000 net investments totalling $125,000. The results in each case can be helpful in deciding when to invest.

These are the results of having invested $5,000 in Templeton Growth Fund, Ltd. for each of the past 25 years on the day the Dow Jones Industrial Average reached its highest point of the year—the <u>peak for stock prices</u> each year.

Date of Market High	Cumulative Investment	Value of Account on December 31
04/28/71	$5,000	$5,305
12/11/72	10,000	13,949
01/11/73	15,000	17,052
03/13/74	20,000	19,045
07/15/75	25,000	31,752
09/21/76	30,000	51,724
01/03/77	35,000	74,451
09/08/78	40,000	100,854
10/05/79	45,000	130,652
11/20/80	50,000	173,452
04/27/81	55,000	176,483
12/27/82	60,000	208,038
11/29/83	65,000	284,830
01/06/84	70,000	314,836
12/16/85	75,000	430,922
12/02/86	80,000	521,119
08/25/87	85,000	498,528
10/21/88	90,000	565,007
10/09/89	95,000	689,198
07/16/90	100,000	599,813
12/31/91	105,000	786,881
06/01/92	110,000	911,131
12/29/93	115,000	1,246,753
01/31/94	120,000	1,299,080
12/13/95	125,000	1,487,888

Average annual compound rate of return: 17.1%

Source: Templeton Management Limited

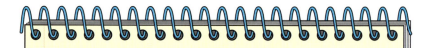

These are the results of having invested $5,000 in Templeton Growth Fund, Ltd. for each of the past 25 years on the day the Dow Jones Industrial Average reached its lowest point of the year—the <u>bottom for stock prices</u> each year.

Date of Market Low	Cumulative Investment	Value of Account on December 31
11/23/71	$5,000	$5,603
01/26/72	10,000	17,181
12/03/73	15,000	20,366
12/06/74	20,000	22,921
01/02/75	25,000	39,380
01/02/76	30,000	64,155
11/02/77	35,000	85,340
02/28/78	40,000	116,733
11/07/79	45,000	151,068
04/21/80	50,000	201,847
09/25/81	55,000	205,394
08/12/82	60,000	243,004
01/03/83	65,000	333,634
07/24/84	70,000	368,235
01/04/85	75,000	504,963
01/22/86	80,000	610,970
10/19/87	85,000	584,624
01/20/88	90,000	662,477
01/03/89	95,000	808,420
10/11/90	100,000	703,988
01/09/91	105,000	917,679
10/09/92	110,000	1,062,069
01/20/93	115,000	1,454,121
04/04/94	120,000	1,514,506
01/30/95	125,000	1,666,805

Average annual compound rate of return: 17.8%

Source: Templeton Management Limited

Most investors would find the results in each case quite acceptable. As a result, it appears that—The "Best" Time to Invest is Whenever You Have The Money!

These illustrations represent the results of net investments. The rate of return and market value of an investment in the Fund will fluctuate, so that shares redeemed may be worth more or less than their original cost. The market is represented by the Dow Jones Industrial Average of 30 Stocks.

THE "BUY AND HOLD" STRATEGY

This approach is similar to dollar cost averaging except that in this strategy, the investment may not be made as regularly.

Assuming you've done your research or had the benefit of the advice of a financial advisor, there's a strong argument for picking a fund, investing the money, and getting on with your life.

Templeton Growth Fund is a classic example of a buy-and-hold fund. A $10,000 investment in this fund in November 1954 — with no subsequent contributions or withdrawals — was worth over $4.1 million in January 1997. You could have been Rip Van Winkle and slept for over 40 years and done very well with Templeton Growth.

But even if your interest is to "buy and hold," we generally aren't comfortable ignoring the investment completely. So to monitor, I suggest you look for changes in the fund's management or for changes to its investment philosophy and, of course, continue to be aware of its performance compared to others in its category.

The buy and hold strategy isn't as exciting as some others, but if you can find a true "buy and hold" fund you'll be a happy investor.

THE "BOB AND WEAVE" STRATEGY

This approach is quite the opposite of "buy and hold" and "dollar cost averaging." It's based on a belief that we as individuals can anticipate certain trends, developments, or events, and can "bob and weave" or switch among funds and asset categories to take advantage of them.

Most fund companies now allow you to switch from one of their funds to another — generally at no cost, although a fund's prospectus often provides for a fee of up to 2%. Some of the no-load funds charge an administration fee each time you do so after a certain number of "free" switches.

Now it's true that certain asset categories tend to do better at different times in the economic cycle. For example, when interest rates are falling, government bonds will tend to do well; when interest rates are low, equities will likely do well; and, when rates are rising, a cash-type investment may perform best.

But I believe very strongly that you should hold a balanced portfolio. So I urge that the "bob and weave" approach not be taken too far. Sure, there could be strategic times to rebalance; but those who attempt to be "market timers" do not consistently come out on top. It's a risky strategy and one that we urge be used with caution — probably as part of ongoing discussions with your financial advisor.

THE ASSET ALLOCATION STRATEGY

The asset allocation approach is a much more disciplined and more effective strategy than the "bob and weave." In this strategy, the overall mix between fixed income and equities is determined by your age and aggressiveness as an investor. (For more about asset allocation, see pages 48-52) Then the specific components of the portfolio are selected and "plugged in" to the overall framework.

Remember, the research shows very clearly that the overall mix between equities and fixed income is the **single most important investment decision we make**. All other variables, including market timing, are of very little importance.

Of course, it will be necessary to rebalance your portfolio from time to time, particularly if one asset category has done extremely well in the past year. If it has, it may have grown to a larger-than-appropriate percentage of the portfolio.

Another reason to adjust your portfolio may be advancing age. I believe that, as we age (and all other things being equal), the relative weighting of fixed-income assets in your portfolio should grow. Some investors become more (or less) aggressive over the years — for a whole variety of reasons — and this change must be reflected in the overall holdings.

Finally as indicated above, certain economic conditions lend themselves to shifts in the weighting of certain asset categories that may not otherwise be appropriate.

The main point here is that changes made to a balanced portfolio should be the result of a well-considered set of plans and have little to do with an attempt to time the market — which is more a part of the "bob and weave" approach.

THE LEVERAGING STRATEGY

This is an aggressive strategy with great upside potential — as well as some significant risk. The theory is to use other people's money — usually a bank loan — adding it to yours and investing the entire amount. What you owe remains constant, or may be reduced by monthly payments, while the overall investment grows in value.

Let's assume you take $20,000 of your own money and borrow another $80,000 to make a $100,000 investment. Let's assume your investment grows by 20% to $120,000. You still owe $80,000, so you "own" $40,000 of the investment. Although the value of the portfolio grew by only 20%, your "stake" actually doubled from $20,000 to $40,000 — a 100% increase!

It can get even better. Assuming you borrowed the money to invest outside your RRSP, the interest you pay the bank to finance the loan will be tax deductible. (Interest on RRSP loans is no longer deductible.) And assuming that you selected investments that generate tax-advantaged dividends or capital gains, your after-tax returns will be better still. (Even though the $100,000 capital gains exemption has been abolished, capital gains are still taxed at only 75% of the amount charged on, say, interest income.)

So far, we've seen only the rosy side of leveraging. But there's another side that must be considered. Let's assume our $100,000 declines in value by 20% to $80,000. That represents the entire amount of your contribution to the total investment. So your original $20,000 will have been wiped out — for a pretty frightening loss of 100%!

Given the potential dangers inherent in leveraging strategies, we suggest that you adhere to the following guidelines:

● borrow to a maximum of 50% of the total investment;

● be sure cash flow will allow ongoing loan payments; don't expect to pay the loan back from profits;

● try to avoid "securing" the loan with other assets, especially your home; unsecured loans are widely available at slightly higher rates (but the interest is fully deductible).

THE INCOME-SPLITTING STRATEGY

SAVE TAXES THROUGH INCOME SPLITTING

THE USUAL SITUATION

	Jim	Peggy
Annual Retirement Income	$100,000	$0.00
Marginal Tax Rate	53.2%	0.00%
Tax Liability	$40,509	$0.00

THE INCOME-SPLITTING STRATEGY

	Jim	Peggy
Annual Retirement Income	$60,000	$40,000
Marginal Tax Rate	50.1%	42.7%
Tax Liability	$19,377	$10,688
Total Tax Liability	$30,065	
Tax Savings: $10,443 after-tax per year		

* Basic personal exemption only

For those who want to reduce their income tax burden, income splitting is very effective.

This simple strategy attempts to take a portion of the earnings attributed to a high-income earner, and place it in the hands of the lower-income spouse. By doing so, many thousands of tax dollars can be saved annually.

Take a look at the chart.

In most cases, as shown in the first example, retirement income is concentrated (if not placed exclusively) in the hands of the higher income earner. By creating and contributing to a spousal RRSP over a number of years, Jim has achieved the same level of retirement income, but it is more evenly split between Jim and Peggy, as the second example shows.

Notice that in the first example, the tax bill is over $40,000, but that in the income-splitting example, the combined tax bill is just over $30,000. This has been achieved by moving Jim to a lower tax bracket so he pays only about $20,000 in tax instead of $40,000. Peggy now pays tax too, but at a lower rate, so she pays about $10,000

That's an after-tax saving of over $10,000 per year! By repeating the scene over and over again, Jim and Peggy can likely save well over $100,000 in taxes over 10 years.

THE TAX EFFICIENT STRATEGY

Tax Efficient/Inefficient Portfolio

Examine the tax inefficient portfolio on the next page. Notice that the bonds are held outside the RRSP and are therefore fully taxed. The stocks held in an equity fund are inside the RRSP and, therefore, tax free. Because the bonds are taxed, the after-tax return is 11.25%.

TAX-INEFFICIENT PORTFOLIO

ASSET CLASS	RRSP	NON-RRSP	TOTAL
Bonds ($100,000 @ 15%)	0	$15,000	$15,000
Stocks ($100,000 @ 15%)	$15,000	0	$15,000
Taxes payable (@ 50%)	0	-$7,500	-$7,500
Total	$15,000	$7,500	$22,500
After-tax return: $22,500/$200,000 = 11.25%			

TAX-EFFICIENT PORTFOLIO

ASSET CLASS	RRSP	NON-RRSP	TOTAL
Bonds ($100,000 @ 15%)	$15,000	0	$15,000
Stocks ($100,000 @ 15%)	0	$15,000	$15,000
Taxes payable (@ 50%)	0	-5,625	-5,625
Total	$15,000	$9,375	$24,375
After-tax return: $24,375/$200,000 = 12.20%			

Now look at the tax efficient portfolio and notice that now, the bonds are held **inside** the RRSP and, therefore, tax free. The equities are held outside the RRSP and even though they are subject to tax, they are taxed more favourably than fixed-income vehicles. The after-tax return in this situation is 12.2%, and while that 1% may not sound like a lot, it becomes very significant as it compounds over the years.

The message is that, where possible, hold assets which are fully taxed (fixed income) inside the RRSP and more favourably taxed assets (equities) outside the RRSP.

WHAT KIND OF FUND IS RIGHT FOR YOU?

LET'S START WITH YOUR AGE

20'S
30'S - 40'S
50'S
60'S - 70'S

No two people have the same investment needs. But there's a good chance that you'll have many of the same needs as people within your age group. So let's start there.

Perhaps you're just completing your education, establishing a home of your own, or starting a family. Either way, you'll have plenty of bills. And you'll need a savings plan to meet these obligations. But if you do have any excess cash, think about putting it into an RRSP or other investment that offers long-term growth potential.

With fewer debts and more assets, you're starting to make some progress. This is the time to be looking at growth oriented "ownership" investments. Why? Because historically, they have offered superior growth rates over the long term.

Your earnings are probably at (or near) their peak. And with the mortgage paid off (as it should be by now), you have more of that income available for investment. Growth is still important, but with retirement in sight, you'll need to start thinking of balancing your fund portfolio with income-producing investments.

Now you're ready to enjoy the rewards of a lifetime's work. Your investment needs will shift more to security and income. But you will still require some growth investments to provide a necessary hedge against inflation.

WEIGH YOUR NEEDS FOR SECURITY, INCOME, AND GROWTH

Considerations based on age, your personal need for security, income, and growth—as well as your tolerance for risk—will also influence your choice of mutual fund. After all, it's not worth investing in a top-performing growth fund if you're going to lie awake at night worrying that it might decline in value.

Basically, it all comes down to understanding yourself, and picking the type of fund that meets your personal needs. To assist in this process, consider the following statements. If you agree with a statement, mark an "x" on the left side of the scale. If you don't agree, mark it on the right. If you're not sure, mark both sides.

AGREE	DISAGREE	
○	○	• Growth is my key investment objective right now. Income is less important.
○	○	• I'm interested in getting some tax relief from my investments.
○	○	• I understand that growth opportunities sometimes involve short-term risk.
○	○	• Investing is a long-term proposition for me. What I buy today, I don't expect to sell tomorrow.
○	○	• I recognize that, historically, "ownership" investments have provided better long-term rates of return than "loanership" investments. I want to be an "owner."

If you agree with all or most of the above statements you tend to be aggressive in your investment outlook. Conversely if you disagree your tendencies are probably conservative.

BALANCING YOUR MUTUAL FUND OBJECTIVES

Conservative

Although you'll probably want to maintain a core portfolio of term deposits and GICs, you may want to investigate the potentially higher returns offered by income-oriented investments such as Money Market Funds, Bond Funds, and Mortgage Funds.

Moderate

Security and income are important to you, but not to the point of excluding the higher potential returns offered by some growth investments. In this case, you should consider Balanced Funds, Asset Allocation Funds, or your own combination of income and growth funds.

Aggressive

You want growth, and you have the time available to achieve it. A little short-term risk doesn't bother you if it means higher potential returns over the long term. You also want more dividends and capital gains in order to improve your after-tax return on non-RRSP investments. To meet these requirements, consider Growth or Equity Funds, and Dividend Funds.

FUNDS DO BETTER

NEW INDEX TELLS BY HOW MUCH

Tempted to abandon mutual funds for the seemingly greener pastures of GICs? Think again. Over the past 20 years, or about four full market cycles, mutual funds have outperformed GICs.

By how much is revealed in the Equion All-Fund Index. It's a composite of all mutual funds in Canada, weighted by each fund size. Dating back to January 1, 1977, the index reveals that mutual funds have averaged an impressive growth of 12.7% compounded annually, while 5-year GICs have on average grown by 9.8% annually in the same period.

In dollar terms, a $1,000 investment in the All-Fund Index at its inception had grown to $10,890 by December 31, 1996, compared with only $6,529 for the average GIC. Updated weekly, the index level is reported in dollars to represent the value today of a $1,000 investment in all mutual funds in Canada at the start of 1977, and it is printed every week in *The Globe and Mail.*

From the index's 20-year history, investors can glean three important lessons. The **first** is that mutual funds "collectively" deliver excellent value. They not only do better than GICs, they have outperformed the TSE stock index including dividends, and they have clobbered inflation. Not just over some lucky period when things were going well, but over a long time, through periods of inflation, deflation, war, recessions, referendums, 20% interest rates, and boom times.

The **second** lesson is that a balanced portfolio is the best blend of risk and return. The All-Fund Index is representative of such a portfolio because it is made up of all funds—equity, bond, resource, international, balance, mortgage and sector funds. (The index excludes money market funds, because they're just another way of holding cash.)

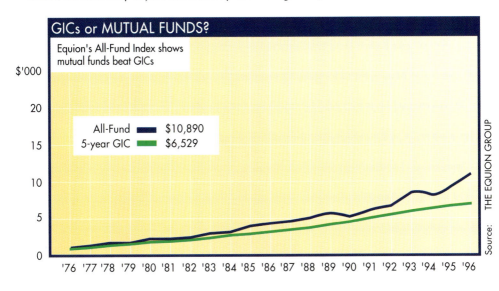

U.S. equity funds have been the best place to be, followed by international equity funds. A $1,000 investment in 1977 is now worth $17,400 in U.S. equity funds. That's an average return of 15.2% annually. Next best were international equity funds at 15.1% annually. But that came with more risk. Specifically, these funds showed about the same volatility as the Canadian stock market and about twice the volatility of Canadian bonds.

A balanced portfolio, however, manages to capture much of the extra return offered by equities without much of the risk. Magic? No, it's just plain math. Because some asset classes zig while others zag, balanced investors enjoy a smoother ride.

As the All-Fund Index shows, investors who diversify earn higher returns, with lower risk. The Index has a standard deviation of 9.1, about a third less risky than the TSE 300 total return index, but it shows a higher rate of return than the TSE. (Standard deviation is a widely used measure of risk.)

The **third** lesson from the 20-year history of the All-Fund Index: Don't even try to time the market. Even during the severe recession of 1980–82, contrary to what you might expect with the benefit of hindsight, the All-Fund Index did well. It rose 35% over that three-year period.

Instead of moving in and out of the market, hang in and put the market to work for you. The All-Fund Index has made money in 17 of the past 20 years, and beaten 5-year GICs in 14 of 20 years.

These types of results aren't an exaggeration of the merit of mutual funds. If anything, the All-Fund Index is a conservative growth yardstick. Because it includes all funds, it is a reasonable indicator of how much you should be able to make without taking big risks, picking strong-performing funds or adding value in any other way.

The truth is, bad funds did exist. But they've been folded, or merged with another fund. When that happens, the poor record vanishes and the merged fund adopts the record of the better fund. The All-Fund Index includes those poor funds, thus avoiding the upward bias of the monthly fund averages.

An index composed of every fund also avoids other selection biases. It doesn't just pick the good performers, or restrict itself to the big funds, which tend to do a little better than the overall fund universe.

In short, the All-Fund Index provides a snapshot of the big picture, something that investors often lose sight of. And the big picture is clear: Funds do better!

THE IMPORTANCE OF ASSET ALLOCATION

What is the most critical factor in successful mutual fund investing? Like many people, you may believe that it all depends on picking the "right" fund — the one with the best numbers. But as most fund managers know, consistently high returns do not depend on putting money into specific securities; rather, it depends on putting money into the right types of securities. The same rule applies to mutual fund investing: put your money into the right fund categories, and chances are you'll be further ahead in the long run.

The categories of funds you choose — and the weighting of each category relative to the portfolio as a whole — is known as **asset allocation**. And Nobel prize-winning research has shown that it accounts for between 85% and 92% of total portfolio returns. (By contrast, the same research puts the contribution of security selection — that is, choice of specific investments — at only about 2%!)

Clearly, the overriding decision in the development of any investment portfolio is the mix of assets within it. Traditionally, however, individual investors have given the **least** consideration to this **most important** decision.

Conversely, the selection of individual components (securities) is of relatively little importance. Yet investors usually spend the most time and energy in making this **least significant** decision.

WHAT ASSET CATEGORIES SHOULD BE INCLUDED?

A well balanced portfolio should include the following:

Fixed-income investments, such as

- ● **Cash or cash equivalents** (CSBs, term deposits, Treasury Bills) to provide liquidity for an emergency or an opportunity
- ● **Canadian bonds** for stability and high income
- ● International bonds for protection against Canadian interest-rate risk

Equity (stock) investments, such as

- ● **Canadian equities**, to participate in our growth via a number of world class Canadian success stories
- ● **International equities**, to hedge the "Canada risk" and for the broadest possible range of investment choices
- ● **Real estate**, for inflation protection with tax benefits and income
- ● **Precious metals**, including gold, for protection from inflation and crisis
- ● **Oil and gas**, for inflation protection with tax benefits and income

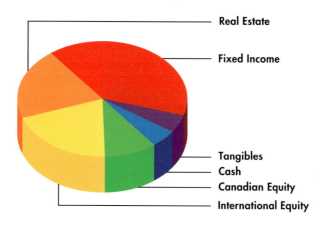

WHAT'S THE RIGHT BALANCE FOR ME?

There is no "perfect" asset mix that's right for every investor. It will vary from person to person, depending on factors such as time horizon, investment objectives, and risk tolerance.

Here are some guidelines that will help you identify the mix that's right for you:

1. Start with your age

   The total percentage of your portfolio held in fixed-income investments (that is, cash and cash equivalents, as well as government and corporate bonds) should approximately match your age. So if you have a $100,000 portfolio and you are 40 years old, about $40,000 should be in fixed income.

2. Assess your risk tolerance

   Imagine a scale ranging from 1 to 10, where a "1" represents the most pathologically cautious, nervous type of investor — the sort of person who keeps his money under the mattress because he's certain the banks will collapse. A "10" is (or would like to be) a professional gambler.

   Which number are you? Our experience is that everyone has an intuitive sense of where they fall on the scale.

3. Adjust your fixed-income percentage

   Here we combine the previous two factors: age and risk tolerance.

   If your risk tolerance is in the middle of the scale at "5", then make no adjustment to the fixed-income component of your portfolio based on your age.

   For every number **higher** than 5, reduce the fixed-income component by 5%. For example, if you are 40 years old and rate yourself a "7" on the risk tolerance scale, reduce your fixed-income component by 10% — in this case, from 40% to 30%.

   For every number **lower** than 5, add 5% to the fixed-income component. For example, if you are 40 years old and rate yourself a "2" on the risk tolerance scale, increase your fixed-income component by 15% — in this case, from 40% to 55%.

   Notice that the effect of these guidelines is to increase the conservative component of your portfolio as you age and become less aggressive.

HOW DO WE KNOW THAT THIS BALANCE WILL WORK?

Well, history is on our side, as you'll see — just study the table below. It outlines the portfolio that's been developed for our 40-year-old investor with 40% fixed income and 60% equity/tangibles in her portfolio. As you'll see, it shows that a balanced portfolio has offered a number of major advantages over the last 19 years.

The bottom line for the balanced portfolio is that it can provide **above-average returns** with **reduced** risk, and offer **preferred tax treatment** at the same time. (See pages 60–65 for more on tax-advantaged mutual fund investing.) My experience is that investors who can obtain all three of these advantages are very happy indeed.

Clearly, there's a lot to be said for developing the right balance among asset categories.

Examine the table outlining the portfolio that has been developed for our 40-year-old investor and note the major advantages of a balanced portfolio over the last 19 years:

1. The average return per year (13%) outperformed several other asset categories.

2. All asset categories except cash and the balanced portfolio showed negative returns in at least one year.

3. Except for cash, the range between the highest and lowest return in any category (i.e., the volatility) was lowest in the balanced portfolio.

RETURNS BY ASSET TYPE

Asset Allocation →	5%	35%	10%	25%	20%	2.50%	2.50%	100%
Year	Cash	Bonds	Canadian Equities	International Equities	Real Estate	Oil & Gas	Gold	Balanced Portfolio
1978	9	4	30	21	12	16	8	13
1979	12	-3	45	14	13	82	91	15
1980	13	7	30	33	23	46	43	21
1981	18	4	-10	-5	26	-29	-38	4
1982	14	35	6	21	1	-14	39	20
1983	9	12	36	25	7	19	-2	16
1984	11	15	-2	12	-19	-20		11
1985	10	21	25	40	10	11	33	24
1986	9	15	9	29	13	-2	29	17
1987	8	4	6	5	14	18	17	7
1988	9	10	11	10	17	-8	-28	10
1989	12	13	21	21	20	25	5	17
1990	13	8	-15	-12	5	-10	1	0
1991	9	22	12	22	0	-9	-12	14
1992	7	10	-1	6	-6	23	2	5
1993	6	18	33	22	-4	68	83	18
1994	5	-4	0	10	2	-12	-3	1
1995	8	21	15	26	5	13	-17	17
1996	5	12	28	19	6	51	22	15
Average	10	12	15	17	9	15	13	13
Variation high to low	13	39	60	52	32	111	129	24
# of years of positive rates	19	17	15	17	17	11	13	19
# of years of negative rates	0	2	4	2	2	8	6	0

Courtesy of The Equion Group

Sources

Cash	91-day Canada T-Bill
Bonds	Scotia McLeod Universe Bond Index prior to 1985 - Scotia McLeod Long Bond Index
Cdn. Equities	TSE 300 Return Index
Int'l Equities	50% Morgan Stanley World Total Return Index, 50% S&P 500
Real Estate	Russell Property Index prior to 1990 - Morguard Property Index
Oil & Gas	AGF Canadian Resource Fund
Gold	Gold Trust Mutual Fund

4. The balanced portfolio outperformed cash on average, and is more favourably taxed than cash.

For many people, a properly balanced portfolio represents the means by which they can participate in the growth and favourable tax treatment of several asset types. At the same time, they enjoy the peace of mind that comes from having an investment which (in our example) has not declined in value during any one of the past nineteen years.

It seems that the caution to not put all your eggs in one basket makes not only "common sense" but also "research sense."

THE IMPORTANCE OF DIVERSIFICATION

A Nobel Prize was awarded recently for research related to investments. The prizewinning conclusion: it's better "not to put all your eggs in one basket"!

Sounds simple, and it is. But what does it mean for individuals and why is it so important?

I've already discussed the concept of a balanced portfolio — where that balance is achieved by weighting your holdings across various asset categories. There are other ways to diversify too, some of which I've discussed earlier in the book.

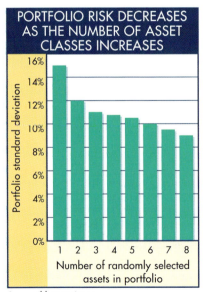

PORTFOLIO RISK DECREASES AS THE NUMBER OF ASSET CLASSES INCREASES

Portfolio standard deviation

Number of randomly selected assets in portfolio

Source: Ibbotson Assoc.

As our portfolio becomes appropriately balanced, it becomes more diversified, and there are major advantages to this diversification.

The accompanying chart shows how diversifying across asset categories helps to reduce risk. Notice that with one asset category in a portfolio (that is, "all your eggs in one basket"), the risk (measured by standard deviation) is about 15%. With each additional asset category, the risk declines so that with representation in 8 asset categories (and there really aren't many more) it's cut almost in half to 9%.

Similarly, when dealing with stocks only, unsystematic risk is substantially reduced by going from owning one stock to owning 128 (although research shows that after 50 stocks are in a portfolio, subsequent additions reduce risk only minimally).

Essentially, diversification is a conservative strategy which acknowledges that we will not always be right in our selection of securities, geographic location or manager; by not overweighting our position in any one of these, the negative impact of being wrong is reduced. Once we acknowledge that we will not be right all the time, we are able to adjust our thinking to achieve more consistent (if less spectacular) growth and avoid big (and potentially) devastating losses.

BE INTERNATIONALLY DIVERSIFIED

Effective diversification is achieved both by holding different asset classes and by investing internationally. The trend to international investing is growing rapidly and with good reason.

To begin with, let's remember that Canada represents only between 2 and 3% of the world's markets. In other words, by restricting our investments to Canada we miss out on the huge opportunities available in the remaining 97% of the world. If you went into a huge supermarket or department store that had 100 different aisles of goods or departments, and were told that you could only shop in 3 of them, you probably wouldn't stand for it. By investing only in Canada, we restrict our choices and it just doesn't make sense.

And let's not forget our debt situation. While concern over it seems to have lessened recently as interest rates have fallen, we need to remember some sobering facts. Our national debt continues to mount by about $85,000 . . . per minute! That's every minute of every hour of every day of every month of every year!

Our debt is currently between about $25,000 and $30,000 . . . for every woman, man, and child in the country. We most definitely have debt problems, which is another reason we don't want to have all our eggs in the "Canada basket".

A third reason we should be investing internationally is demonstrated by the chart on page 54. It clearly shows that stock markets in several other countries have outperformed ours over the last 20 years. Furthermore, there's no really strong reason to believe that this trend won't continue. Not only then does the world offer a wider range of choices for investment than are available in Canada, other parts of the world have delivered better returns to investors.

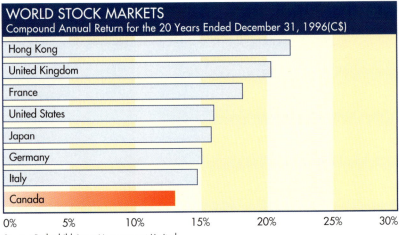

WORLD STOCK MARKETS
Compound Annual Return for the 20 Years Ended December 31, 1996(C$)

Hong Kong	
United Kingdom	
France	
United States	
Japan	
Germany	
Italy	
Canada	

0%   5%   10%   15%   20%   25%   30%

Source: Rothschild Asset Management Limited

We also need to invest internationally because we can not only improve our returns, but actually reduce our risk at the same time. Now isn't that the goal of every investor? As the accompanying chart shows, by holding varying portions of our portfolio outside Canada we can achieve both goals at the same time.

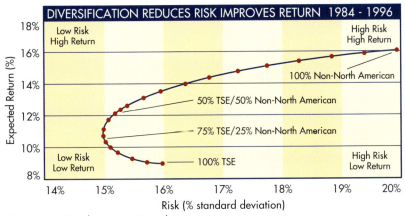

DIVERSIFICATION REDUCES RISK IMPROVES RETURN 1984 - 1996

Low Risk High Return

High Risk High Return

100% Non-North American

50% TSE/50% Non-North American

75% TSE/25% Non-North American

Low Risk Low Return

100% TSE

High Risk Low Return

Expected Return (%): 8% 10% 12% 14% 16% 18%

Risk (% standard deviation): 14% 15% 16% 17% 18% 19% 20%

Source: Loring Ward Investment Counsel

Finally, we need to consider holding at least a portion of our portfolio in the emerging markets as shown in the chart on page 55. These "emerging markets" constitute 77% of the world's land area and 85% of the world's population...but only about 25% of the world's gross domestic product (GDP).

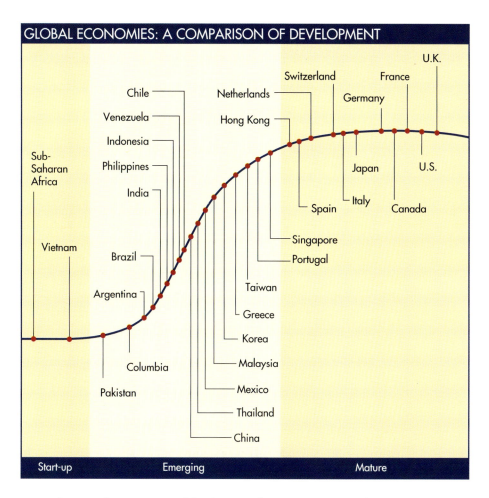

GLOBAL ECONOMIES: A COMPARISON OF DEVELOPMENT

Start-up   Emerging   Mature

As these markets mature and begin to produce a proportionately greater share of world GDP, the investment returns are likely to be very attractive. But don't get too heavily invested in the emerging markets. By definition they are immature by Western standards and can therefore be particularly volatile.

KEEP AN EYE ON INTEREST RATES

There is a multitude of economic indicators used to predict the direction of the economy. Everything from housing starts, to unemployment figures, to car sales and the price of gold is considered. For most of us, it's really very complicated.

Well here's a way to simplify the exercise by concentrating on one vital indicator: interest rates. It's not foolproof, but it can be very helpful.

Generally, high interest rates have a positive impact on savings, GICs, Treasury Bills, mortgages (if you hold mortgages) and bonds. Conversely, high interest rates have a negative impact on businesses (borrowing costs are higher), stocks, and real estate.

Low interest rates reverse the situation and exert a negative impact on savings, GICs, Treasury Bills, mortgages (if you are a mortgage holder) and bonds, while exerting a much more positive influence on businesses (which can expand more easily on borrowing costs that are lower), stocks, and real estate.

Using this understanding of interest rates can help us to identify investment opportunities. Let's consider the current situation.

Compared to the last 20 years, interest rates are quite low today: prime is at 4.75% (at the time of writing); 5-year GICs offer about 4.4%; CSBs pay 5.2%; T-Bills are about 3.7%; and savings accounts are under 1.0%!

In keeping with our understanding of interests rates, as they have declined recently, Canadian equities have been moving ahead nicely and Canadian equity mutual funds have averaged growth of over 24.6% over the last year and 11.1% over the last 3 years (January 31, 1997).

Similarly, we might also want to be considering investments in real estate. While real estate in most parts of the country continues to languish, it's quite likely that continued low interest rate levels will have a ripple effect—from enabling business expansion/creation to ultimately, recovery and growth in the real estate sector.

Clearly many factors impact upon an economic cycle and determine which asset categories will experience growth. But those who pay attention to interest rate movements can often anticipate areas of future opportunity.

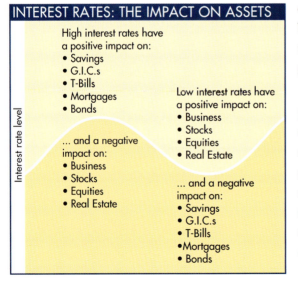

INTEREST RATES: THE IMPACT ON ASSETS

Interest rate level

High interest rates have a positive impact on:
• Savings
• G.I.C.s
• T-Bills
• Mortgages
• Bonds

... and a negative impact on:
• Business
• Stocks
• Equities
• Real Estate

Low interest rates have a positive impact on:
• Business
• Stocks
• Equities
• Real Estate

... and a negative impact on:
• Savings
• G.I.C.s
• T-Bills
•Mortgages
• Bonds

CHAPTER 3

ad to say, most Canadians pay more income tax than necessary — in many cases, a lot more!

As I said earlier, it's largely because they don't know the rules of the tax game, and they therefore play the game poorly. To make it even worse, many accountants (to whom we often look for assistance in this regard) see their job as to calculate the amount of tax we owe, rather than to educate their clients so they can plan wisely to reduce their tax burden.

We'll outline some of the best tax saving strategies for individuals a little later, but for now, look at this example.

Which would you prefer?

	A	B
Rate of return	16.0 %	16 %
Taxes (40%)	– 6.4 %	0 %
Inflation (5% average)	– 5.0 %	– 5 %
Real Rate of Return	= 4.6 %	= 11 %

Obviously you'd prefer a real rate of return of 11.0% rather than 4.6%. Who wouldn't?

Coach's Quote

"Next to being shot at and missed, there's nothing quite as satisfying as a big tax refund."

Notice that in our example, the only difference between A and B is in the amount of tax paid. How do you pay zero tax on an investment? Simple. Buy a Registered Retirement Savings Plan. As long as your money remains inside your RRSP, you pay no tax on it. It grows much more rapidly, and you're getting a much better real rate of return than you would otherwise.

Note that your investment goals of growth and tax relief are not mutually exclusive. Quite the opposite — they fit beautifully together in an RRSP.

EVERYBODY HAS A TAX PROBLEM

Earlier I pointed out how in 1996, 46% of the income of an average Canadian family was paid out in taxes of all sorts. I also showed how Tax Freedom Day, the day in the year when the average Canadian has paid all the taxes he or she owes to all levels of government doesn't occur until July.

You'll also remember that tax relief is one of the three key financial objectives for Canadians and that we should take advantage of tax breaks made available to us.

RETIREMENT REALITY

Retirement reality is often shockingly different from retirement dreaming or fantasizing. In the next few years, Canada will experience a dramatic increase in the number of seniors. As a result, there is no guarantee that social programs once considered universal will be continued. There is no contract with the government; programs can be wiped out. With so much doubt surrounding both employer pensions and public old age security programs, growing numbers of Canadians are concluding that their most reliable source of retirement will likely be their RRSPs.

It's clear then that saving for retirement is an absolute necessity for every Canadian and that we cannot rely on the government to take care of us in a way that will allow us to maintain our standard of living at the level we wish.

Over and over again, statistics show that many Canadians retire near or even below the poverty level. Hundreds of thousands of Canadians including professionals, sales people working on commission, owners of businesses, and employees of businesses — in fact nearly 60% of Canadians — do not belong to a pension plan. Nearly 50% of retired Canadians require some form of government assistance to survive!

Despite these scary facts, other statistics show in study after study that Canadians have the naive belief that somehow or other, the money they need in retirement will miraculously be there to allow them to live at the level to which they've become accustomed.

Remember, the reasonable goal for every Canadian should be to retire at the same income level as enjoyed in his or her peak earning years.

Let's say that Jack Cooper earns a salary of $50,000 in his final year at work. How much money would he need to have saved to achieve the goal of enjoying an income of $50,000 in retirement? If we assume a 10% return on his money, you can see that he would require a nest egg of $500,000 to achieve this goal ($500,000 × 10% = $50,000.) That's a lot of money!

Approximately 40% to 45% of Canadians contribute to pension plans, some of which are very good, providing 60% to 70% of the final year's salary. But even these people need to be putting aside money to make up that 30% to 40% shortfall.

Again, let's take the example of Jill Bowman who retires with a pension of 65% of her final year's salary; let's assume she was earning $60,000 in that final year. Her pension then would be about $40,000 and she'd need to ensure an extra income of $20,000 to achieve her goal. At a 10% return on her money, she would need about $200,000 in savings ($200,000 × 10% = $20,000).

Now some will say that in retirement, expenses are lower and that you don't need the same amount of income. I suppose there are some who go from work to retirement in a rocking chair, but I don't know many. My experience is that they're equally likely to be travelling, playing golf, or getting involved in a variety of sports or hobby activities — all of which cost money. Many people put off major trips until their retirement, when they'll have the time to go. But will they have the money? Don't accept the idea that you'll need less in retirement. It's not a necessary situation, but to avoid it you must plan ahead.

If all of this information about the amount of money required in retirement is depressing, let me now tell you the good news — and it is good news indeed. Not only will the government subsidize your RRSP contribution (in some cases over 50%) by allowing it as a deduction, it also allows the money to grow tax free as long as it's in the RRSP. Two fantastic advantages! And to make it even better, the government has recently raised RRSP contribution limits in a way that will be advantageous to thousands and thousands of Canadians.

AN RRSP IS THE SOLUTION

Here are three key advantages of an RRSP.

1. Increased contribution limits

Starting in 1991, RRSP contribution limits for those who do not belong to a pension plan were increased to the lesser of 18% of earned income or $11,500. Higher limits planned for 1996 to 2005 are shown below.

RRSP CONTRIBUTION LIMITS

For those who do not contribute to a pension plan at work, the maximum RRSP contribution is 18% of earned income or the following, whichever is less:

1996–2003	$13,500
2004	$14,500
2005	$15,500

Contribution limits are based on earned income for the previous year. Those who contribute to a pension plan at work are required to calculate a Pension Adjustment (P.A.). It's complicated, but fortunately the P.A. is indicated on your T4 slip.

2. Tax savings

The total amount contributed comes directly "off the top" of your income for tax purposes and can therefore significantly reduce the amount of income tax you pay each year.

For example, if you had earned income of $50,000 in 1996, you can contribute up to $9,000 in your RRSP in 1997 (the lesser of $13,500 or 18% of earned income; 18% of $50,000 = $9,000). This means your earned income for tax purposes is $41,000. You would be approximately in the 42% tax bracket and would therefore get a tax saving in 1997 of about $3,780 (42% of $9,000). Now we're talking!

3. Tax-free growth

While the money you invest stays in the RRSP, it grows tax free. Using the Rule of 72, we can quickly calculate that at 12% it would double in only six years. Outside the RRSP and subject to tax at 42%, your investment would take over nine years to double.

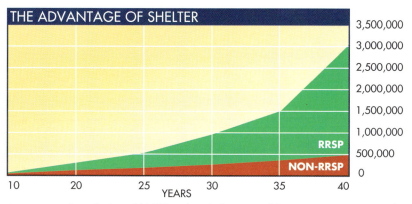

Assumes annual contributions of $3,500 made at the beginning of the year; 12% average annual compound rate of return; 45% combined federal-provincial tax rate.

START EARLY!

Diane opens an RRSP at 12%, invests $2,000 per year for six years, and then stops. She makes no further contributions to the RRSP for the next 38 years.

Jim spends $2,000 per year for six years on himself, then opens an RRSP and contributes $2,000 per year at 12% for the next 38 years.

See what happens! At age 65, Diane, who has invested only $12,000 has accumulated nearly as much as Jim, who has invested $76,000.

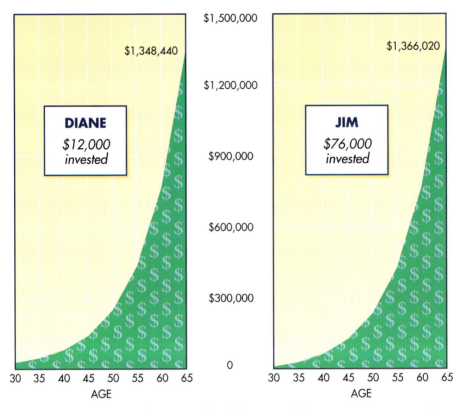

Assumes annual contributions of $2,000 made at the beginning of the year; 12% average annual compound rate of return.

Money Coach Rule

Start early and make the maximum RRSP contribution every year! Let time, compounding, and tax free growth in an RRSP work hard for you!

CONTRIBUTE MONTHLY

We've already encouraged you to use the Dollar Cost Averaging strategy, and examined the advantages of doing so. But there is another advantage in investing in your RRSP monthly rather than in a lump sum annually. For most people, it's just easier to find a smaller amount monthly than a larger amount annually . . . usually in February when you're still facing Christmas bills.

However, the major advantage is that you'll likely earn more by investing monthly. The following chart sums it up very succinctly.

Does $32,000 extra make it sound attractive? It should!

MONTHLY VS. ANNUAL CONTRIBUTIONS

(Using 12% Sample Rate)

$455,606	$423,315
$500 Monthly	$6,000 Annually

By contributing $500 monthly ($500 x 12 = $6,000) to an RRSP earning 12%, over 20 years, you would be left with $32,000 more than by contributing $6,000 annually at year end over the same period.

WHERE CAN YOU INVEST YOUR RRSP DOLLARS?

There is a wide range of options available for your RRSP. They include savings accounts, Canada Savings Bonds, Treasury Bills, Canadian government and corporate bonds, Guaranteed Investment Certificates, term deposits, shares listed on certain Canadian stock exchanges, and a growing number of mutual funds that fulfill prescribed Canadian ownership limits. There are other possibilities as well, but these are the major ones.

In the past, banks, trust companies, and life insurance companies have dominated the RRSP market, offering their "loanership" vehicles. Recently, however, as more and more people have come to learn the advantages and benefits of "ownership," mutual funds have become very popular as RRSP investments.

Money Coach Rule

I believe that for most people, a mutual fund selected to meet their investment objectives of growth, tax relief, and security should be the investment of choice because I believe that selected ownership will outperform loanership over the long term as it has in the past.

TAKE ADVANTAGE OF FOREIGN CONTENT RULES

Canada makes up only about 3% of the world's markets, so it makes good sense to diversify our investments and take advantage of the growth opportunities available in the other 97% of the world's markets.

Current Revenue Canada rules allow us to hold up to 20% of our RRSP in foreign content investments outside Canada.

The following is a great way to increase the foreign content of your RRSP beyond the stated limits. It's an approach that works best with a self-directed RRSP.

Begin by taking full advantage of the 20% allowed for the foreign part of your ("direct") contributions.

Then, invest the non-foreign ("indirect") portion of your RRSP contribution in a mutual fund that qualifies as Canadian property but takes full advantage of the foreign content limits. The following example demonstrates how we can increase our foreign content component significantly.

Let's assume for simplicity, that you can contribute $10,000 to your RRSP. This means that $2,000 of the contribution (20%) can be invested in foreign holdings.

This leaves 8,000 to be invested in non-foreign investments. However, if you were to invest that $8,000 in a Canadian mutual fund which, in itself, has 20% of its holdings in foreign investments, it means that 20% of your $8,000 (i.e., $1,600) is also being invested outside the country. Therefore, you have increased your foreign investments to $3,600 ($2,000 +$1,600) or 36% of your contribution.

CONSIDER A SPOUSAL RRSP

A spousal RRSP is registered in the name of one spouse, but the contributions have come from the other spouse. These plans are particularly appropriate in a situation where one spouse may be at home and not earning much taxable income, and the other spouse is in a high tax bracket.

Let's say that Robert is earning a good salary and that his wife Michelle is at home raising a family. The strategy would be for Robert to contribute, let's say, $1,000 to an RRSP in Michelle's name — a spousal RRSP. Robert gets to claim the $1,000 deduction immediately, but when the funds are withdrawn in the future, they are taxed in Michelle's name. This is great for both of them since Robert, being in a higher tax bracket saves taxes now. Michelle, who will pay the tax on withdrawal, will likely be in a lower tax bracket and therefore pay less tax than Robert would if it were added to his already solid pension income.

SPOUSE AS BENEFICIARY

An important consideration if you are married is to name your spouse as beneficiary of your RRSP. If you do, the money can be transferred to your spouse's RRSP on your death and remain there tax free until he or she deregisters the plan. If you don't name your spouse as beneficiary, the RRSP will be included as income on your tax return in the year of your death and a substantial tax bill could result. Keep it in the family and don't let the government get any more taxes than necessary!

THE ULTIMATE RRSP STRATEGY: A GROUP PLAN

Recently, group RRSPs have started to become popular. Basically a group RRSP is a series of individual RRSPs held by people who all work for the same employer.

The main advantage of a group RRSP for the individual is that (in addition to all the other advantages of an RRSP) where monthly payroll deductions are made by the employer, the employee's taxes are automatically reduced. For example, a person in the 40% tax bracket contributing $300 per month in a group RRSP saves $120 per month in income tax and doesn't have to wait until income tax filing time to claim their deduction and get their rebate.

Money Coach Rule

An early start on an RRSP is one of the best investments you can make, because it achieves all three investment goals: growth, tax relief, security.

Of course, when we have a chance to get money from Revenue Canada now or later — get it now! For many people, this "forced saving" is the difference between contributing to the RRSP and not doing so. Check to see if there's a group plan available where you work. If so, join it. If not, ask about setting one up. It's simple to do.

THE BAD NEWS ABOUT RRSPs

I believe that the RRSP, which has now been in place in Canada since about 1957, is the greatest thing since sliced bread!

But you know what? We're not using it nearly to full advantage.

A recent study showed that only about 50% of Canadians actually have an RRSP and that we're contributing on average, only about 13% of what we could contribute and claim a tax deduction!

It gets worse! Another recent study determined that to fund a 25-year retirement, an individual requires about $525,000. The size of the average RRSP today is about $30,100.

We've got a lot of work to do and we'd better get started fast . . . because the government simply will not be able to afford to provide the pension incomes many of us are naively expecting.

· RRSP REPLAY ·

We've seen that many concepts I've been urging you to use thus far, are activated when you start an RRSP.

- Ideally you'll begin as soon as you start earning an income.
- You'll be an owner (through purchase of mutual funds) rather than a loaner.
- You'll use the Rule of 72 to calculate the time it'll take for your investment to double and always seek the highest rate of growth (that's consistent with reasonable security).
- You'll let the magic of compounding work for you.
- You'll invest a fixed amount monthly using dollar cost averaging.
- You'll get tax relief as a result of purchasing an RRSP.

OTHER STRATEGIES FOR SAVING INCOME TAX

I have commented throughout the book on the importance of taxes — particularly income tax. Taxes almost invariably get in the way of our achieving the return on our investments that we'd like. That's why it's important to be aware of opportunities available to legally reduce the amount of tax we pay. That process is called tax planning; it's the minimizing of the amount we pay in income tax through the proper handling of our financial affairs.

With our government debt continuing to grow at about $85,000 per minute, and with no realistic likelihood of this situation drastically changing any time soon, two key trends are likely to emerge. *First,* government services will have to be cut. This will likely include chops to education funding (thus throwing a larger financial burden on students and their parents) and increasing "clawbacks" to government pensions and payments.

Second, it's a virtual **certainty** that taxes of all types will rise in Canada in the future. Some predict that the marginal tax rate now at about 53% maximum will rise to 70%! We can also expect "temporary" surtaxes . . . which will become permanent. And we can expect the GST currently at 7% to rise to levels similar to the VAT (value added tax) rate of 25% in Germany and 26% in Ireland.

For these reasons, we must get better at tax planning . . . using every legal means available to reduce the amount we pay. Canadians are strange. We pay high taxes and complain bitterly about it; but we don't actually explore all the opportunities to reduce our burden.

Tax planning involves using our knowledge of the rules, put in place by the government, to look for opportunities to reduce our taxable income. RRSPs are among the very best examples. Tax planning usually involves the assistance of a person whose judgement we trust, in whom we have confidence, and who is knowledgeable about the current tax rules . . . sounds like we're describing a money coach!

Tax planning is very different from tax evasion, which is illegal and which brings with it severe penalties including fines and possibly a jail term.

So, in addition to maximizing your RRSP contributions, how else can you save taxes? While there are tax saving opportunities available to individuals depending on their unique circumstances (e.g., business owners, the self employed, commissioned salespeople), the following are among the favourite and best tax savings strategies available to most Canadians today:

DIVIDEND VS. INTEREST INCOME

Faced with a choice, we can save substantial income tax by electing to receive dividend or capital gains income, rather than interest income. Here's how.

Let's assume we are receiving $1,000 of investment income in the form of interest. This is what Canadians often do, because they often hold a majority of their investments in cash, CSBs, T-Bills, etc., and these investments pay interest. Let's also assume for each example that you are in the 50% marginal tax bracket. In this case, as the chart shows, your $1,000 is divided so that $500 goes to Revenue Canada and $500 comes to you. Revenue Canada thinks that's fair; you work for the money and give them half! Do you?

THE EFFECT REVENUE CANADA HAS ON $1,000 OF INVESTMENT INCOME

	$1,000 of Interest Income	$1,000 of Dividend Income	$1,000 of Capital Gains Income
Tax Rate @ 50%	$500	$360	$375
After-Tax Income	$500	$640	$625

We could reduce our tax bite if we chose to receive dividend income, rather than interest income. The government encourages us to invest in Canadian corporations by giving us a "dividend tax credit" — a tax break. Often companies that pay dividends are large, conservative, blue chip operations like the banks, which make huge profits, so there seems little risk in investing there.

In our example, you'll see that $1,000 of dividend income is divided more favourably; about $360 to Revenue Canada and $640 to you.

A third option is to invest in areas where the profits are taxed as "capital gains". Many people are of the mistaken impression that when the $100,000 lifetime capital gains exemption was ended in 1994, there was no future tax advantage in capital gains. Wrong! Now, 75% of any capital gains is taxed at your marginal rate, but 25% continues to be available tax free.

In our example, $1,000 of capital gains would carry a tax of about $375, leaving $625 for you, the person who earned it.

So it's important to be up to date on the tax rules as you play the "money game". It can mean extra money in your pocket.

NO ATTRIBUTION ON CAPITAL GAINS WITH MINORS

If you invest money in trust for a minor in an interest bearing investment, not only will you get comparatively low returns but you'll also be delighted to know that the interest earned is attributable to you. You must pay tax on it! That's why CSBs and bank accounts aren't great for this purpose.

A better alternative is to invest in a capital gains seeking investment such as an international equity mutual fund. First you'll likely get much better return. But second, any capital gains are attributed to the minor, not to you. The result? No tax will likely be due.

CLAIM APPROPRIATE BUSINESS EXPENSES

If you are operating a small personal business, most expenses that are paid out in the course of doing business or for the purpose of developing the business, can be used as deductions that may have the effect of reducing the amount of personal income tax you pay. This includes a salary that may be paid for work done by a spouse or child.

LIMITED PARTNERSHIP INVESTMENTS

These investments, sometimes called "tax shelters," allow the investor to claim tax deductions, often of up to $20,000 per year, that can be applied to offset income from other sources — usually earned income.

Such investments have become so popular and are now so much a part of the mainstream of Canadian investment that they are now referred to specifically on our federal income tax return forms.

Such investments, even after the tax deductions are taken into account, sometimes require an annual out-of-pocket, after-tax expense to the investor. It's important to note that these are investments first and tax shelters second. They should be seen as such and should not be purchased primarily because they save tax.

You will have to do your homework, ask probing questions, read accompanying sales materials and legal documentation carefully, and ask for your advisor's opinion.

Limited partnerships come in many forms. In some cases, the limited partners invest in the production of movies or television series; in others they fund mining ventures for oil and gas.

Traditionally, the most popular limited partnerships are land-based, and range from the construction of residential townhouses or highrise apartments to commercial shopping plazas, or nursing homes. Limited partnerships that represent ownership in well located and fairly priced real estate still provide excellent opportunities for growth, tax relief, and security.

Venture Capital Funds

Over the last several years, attractive tax deductions have been offered to people who invest in labour-sponsored venture capital funds. These funds are intended to provide financing to smaller companies that may have found traditional financing difficult. In addition to the usual deductions allowed to RRSP investors, venture capital funds offered attractive additional deductions made available by several provincial governments. The result was that there were total tax credits available of up to 40%. Unfortunately, one fund abused the rules by investing too slowly and allowing cash to pile up in low returning T-Bill accounts.

As a result, governments have cracked down on all labour-sponsored funds. Recent rules require that they be 70% invested by December 31, 1997. As well, the total tax credits available have been reduced to about 30% (depending on the province), and the holding period has been extended from five to eight years. Investors who sell their funds before the required hold period ends will have their tax savings reclaimed.

As well, these funds have not generally provided particularly strong returns when compared to some of the better Canadian mutual funds. And to make things worse, their expense ratios often run at about 4.5%—about twice the level of a typical Canadian equity mutual fund. This high cost eats into already generally modest returns.

On the other hand, some of them have attracted strong management teams, and provided opportunities for Canadians to invest and assist in the growth of exciting new Canadian ventures. They also still provide additional tax deductions above and beyond those provided by traditional RRSPs so that under the new rules, a $3,500 investment can produce maximum combined federal and provincial tax credits of $1,050.

The 1997 Federal Budget introduced incentives to induce labour-sponsored venture capital corporations to invest greater amounts into smaller businesses, i.e., those with less than $10 million of assets.

Oil and Gas Limited Partnerships

For those seeking extra tax advantages, ongoing tax favoured income, the potential for capital gain and who at the same time wish to add a tangible asset to their portfolio, an oil and gas limited partnership investment may be appropriate.

One of the most popular of this type is the annual NCE Oil and Gas Fund Partnership, and in a nutshell, here's how it works.

The minimum investment is $12,500 with $7,500 due on subscription and the remainder due on March 31 of the following year. The investment is 100% deductible over about 5 years and provides regular quarterly tax sheltered income for the life of the project, projected to be 10 years.

The primary risk of the investment appears to be the possibility of a long term decline in world oil and gas prices. However, given that there are no new known world oil or gas reserves of consequence, combined with the ever growing demand for oil and gas, especially in some of the world's emerging and rapidly growing economies, the likelihood of a long term decline in price seems remote to many industry analysts.

On the upside, rising prices may well increase the quarterly dividend and allow a sale of contracts held by the company at higher prices in the future.

Many people also see the addition of tangible assets such as oil and gas to a portfolio as a prudent strategy. Historically, oil and gas have acted as a hedge against inflation, rising in price when stock and bond prices decline. As well, oil prices are denominated in US dollars and much Canadian gas is exported denominated in US dollars too, thus offering further diversification to the portfolio.

Remember your priorities

Don't lose sight of the priorities! Tax shelters should generally only be considered after you've paid off most or all of your mortgage, after you've made your annual RRSP contribution, after you've paid off virtually all outstanding loans, after you've got a growing 10% fund, and when you're earning substantial annual income. They're not for everybody, but at the right time and for the right person, they can be very attractive investments.

ASSIGN LIMITED PARTNERSHIP INCOME TO A SPOUSE

" "

Coach's Quote

"Paying less income tax is not the privilege of the rich; it's the plan of the wise"

If you invest in a limited partnership and receive income from it, the income will be taxed in your hands, at your marginal tax rate. This rate will presumably be near the top bracket.

One way to reduce taxes is to assign such income to a lower tax bracket spouse. He or she will pay tax at their lower rate, resulting in what could be considerable savings.

CONSIDER A FAMILY TRUST

While family trust legislation has changed to be somewhat less attractive over the past several years, there may still be situations in which the creation of a family or an offshore trust may be appropriate.

For more information on the use of trusts, see page 114.

MAKE YOUR MORTGAGE PAYMENTS TAX DEDUCTIBLE

In certain situations, it may be possible to convert your non-deductible mortgage payments to deductible payments. Here's one situation where it can work.

Let's assume you have an investment (non-RRSP) portfolio valued at $200,000 and that at the same time you have a $200,000 mortgage.

The strategy works like this: Sell your investments and use the funds and pay off the mortgage. Then, set up another $200,000 mortgage as collateral to repurchase your $200,000 investment portfolio. The result is that interest on the loan, now taken for investment purposes, can be claimed as a tax deduction.

Assuming interest payments on it of about $10,000 annually, this strategy can result in tax savings at the 50% tax bracket of about $5,000 per year!

KEEP UP TO DATE

These suggestions can be valuable as you try to take advantage of the income tax rules. But remember, the rules keep changing, and it's important to do your best to keep up with the changes that affect you. Large Canadian newspapers are giving increasing attention to business and financial matters, so I suggest you read papers like *The Financial Post*, *The Globe and Mail*, or the business section of your daily newspaper. In addition, a growing number of business magazines are available to help inform and entertain.

CHAPTER 4

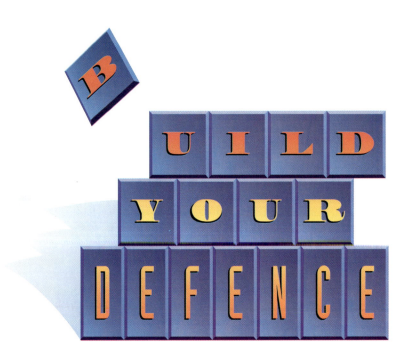

BUILD YOUR DEFENCE

ecurity is definitely a vital investment objective and one which is taken seriously by virtually every investment manager.

Security is often achieved through "guarantees" offered by financial institutions which guarantee rates of interest to be paid to investors over various periods of time. The following instruments offer guarantees: term deposits, Guaranteed Investment Certificates, Canada Savings Bonds, mortgage-backed securities, and others.

Further security is offered to Canadians by the Canada Deposit Insurance Corporation (CDIC), which guarantees most deposits up to $60,000 against the default of the bank or trust company (but not credit union) that holds your funds.

But there is definitely a price to be paid for this security. For the most part, as described earlier, the price is a lower real rate of return paid by the bank or trust company. At best, you're treading water and it's probably fair to say that you'll never get rich by putting all your money in the bank.

As Canadians, we have traditionally craved security and guarantees. Every year we lend millions of dollars to the Government of Canada by buying what some people call Canada Sucker Bonds — CSBs. We deposit billions of dollars with banks, trust companies and insurance companies, and make them rich.

Of course security is important, and there is a place for "guaranteed" financial products in almost everyone's plan. But perhaps we should more often do what the banks and insurance companies do with our money once we've lent it to them at guaranteed, but comparatively low, rates of return. They invest it in mortgages and real estate, making higher rates of return, and keeping the difference for themselves.

In this section we'll take a look at how you can build your financial defence.

• COACH'S PLAYBOOK •

Establish an emergency fund

Many financial planners and advisors suggest that you establish an emergency fund equal to about three months' salary. For many people, that's an amount in the $10,000 range. But if this amount is sitting in a savings account, it's earning low rates of interest, and the interest earned is fully taxable. I believe it's far better to use the money to pay down your mortgage, pay off consumer debt, or "top up" your RRSP.

I believe that an emergency fund is worthwhile, but I feel that $5,000 should generally be the maximum amount you hold in cash. It's great to have a few thousand dollars available whenever you want it. You'll no doubt sleep better at night

knowing you've got money in the bank, and knowing that you can act quickly if you see a really great bargain. But don't get carried away!

The alternative I recommend is that if you're concerned about needing cash quickly, you establish a line of credit in an amount from $3,000 to $10,000 or more with your local bank manager.

A line of credit for $3,000 means that you can write a cheque or cheques for up to that amount whenever you want even though you do not actually have the money in your account. You pay interest only on the amount actually used (e.g., you may write a cheque for $1, 000 on a $3,000 line of credit; you pay interest only on the $1,000 amount). A line of credit, used effectively, can be a very valuable financial tool. Just be sure you pay it off as quickly as you can, particularly if you have used it for a consumer product, i.e., a car, stereo, trip, etc.

By establishing a line of credit, you can be sure money will be there if you need it and, at the same time, you'll be free to invest your assets in more productive ways.

BE IT EVER SO HUMBLE, THERE'S NO PLACE LIKE HOME . . . ESPECIALLY IF IT'S PAID OFF

For many people, their home has been their very best investment. Depending on when they bought and what downpayment they had, they've probably made a solid return of between 10% and 15% average annual compound rate on their money. In dollar figures, most peoples' homes have increased substantially if not dramatically over the last 25 years.

For this and several other reasons, most Canadians seem to prefer home ownership.

● While it's true that there is some risk involved in the purchase of real estate, and while it's certainly not guaranteed that prices will steadily increase forever, I believe that if you choose a suitable location in an area with a diversified economy and hold your property over the long term, your home will increase in value. One recent study in Ontario confirmed that over a 30-year period, residential housing provided an average annual compound return of 11.95%. While no investments are "perfect," home ownership is probably in the "excellent" category.

● In addition to a reasonable rate of return, your principal residence is completely tax free on sale, which means that the real rate of return (average annual rate minus taxes…in this case zero…minus inflation) is likely to be somewhere around 5% to 10%, which is excellent.

You'll remember earlier I said that anything above a 3% real rate of return is outstanding. Because all the growth is tax free, some people accurately consider their home to be the ultimate tax shelter.

● As well, the home symbolizes many of the true joys of life: children born and raised, happy holiday memories around a fireplace or by the pool. A home is far more than an investment; it's a way of life to the extent that many people don't even consider their home as anything other than a home. For most, even though they don't recognize it, it's far more than a place to live, and the phrase "joy of owning your own home" has more than one meaning.

● My grandfather used to say that the best way to save is to be forced to — through debt. Most people who buy a home today have some debt on it in the form of a mortgage. And most take their mortgage payments seriously (or they should). Thus a home can be seen as the ultimate in forced savings. Bit by bit the mortgage is paid off, and ultimately, we not only own the home outright, but are delighted to discover that it's worth far more than it was when we bought it!

" "

Coach's Quote

"If you think nobody cares if you're alive, try missing a couple of mortgage payments."

It's clear that there are many good reasons for purchasing if possible. But even if you do not purchase a home, it's not the end of the world! Certainly the place you live can be a centre of years of happy family activity whether it's rented or owned. And don't forget this ideal of home ownership is primarily a North American phenomenon. Millions and millions of people throughout the world rent rather than own their home or apartment and are content doing so.

But if we look at the owned home as a good investment, how can a renter achieve similar growth? Let's assume that Don can rent an apartment for $1,000 a month or buy it for $1,350 a month in mortgage costs — the difference is $350 per month. If Don rented all his life and invested the $350 (in addition to his 10% fund), he'd be in a very healthy financial condition. Remember the power of compounding over the long term? The difficulty might be that while he'd be forced to make the $1,350 payment monthly or lose the apartment, he might not be disciplined enough to set that extra $350 per month aside for 20 or 25 years.

Home ownership has really paid off!

According to a recent study by Clayton Research Associates, home ownership in Canada has proved to be an excellent investment over the 30 years from 1961 to 1991. The study sampled families who purchased homes at various times during the 30-year period — in St. John's, Halifax, Saint John, Charlottetown, Quebec City, Toronto, London, Winnipeg, Regina, Edmonton, and Victoria — and compared their average financial position with that of people who chose to pay rent and invest the equivalent of a down payment. Because the study was based on long-term trends which have not fundamentally changed since 1991, Clayton believes its findings are still valid even though the study has not been updated.

Here are some of the findings:

A significantly higher net worth among homeowners — $139,000 higher after 20 years, and $198,000 higher after 30 years.

In the future, home ownership will probably continue to be a good investment. Assuming inflation stays low at 2%, the Clayton study forecasts that homeowners will still be worth some $50,000 more than renters in 20 years, and $167,000 more after 30 years.

PAY DOWN THE MORTGAGE FAST: HERE'S HOW

If you buy a home and have a mortgage, it probably represents your single biggest monthly commitment. It is also paid completely in after-tax dollars. ("After-tax dollars" means that every dollar paid off against your mortgage has already been taxed. So depending on your tax rate, you have to earn between $1.40 and $1.50 to pay off every dollar of your mortgage.) That's painful, and it's one reason to pay off your mortgage as quickly as you can.

The second reason you should pay off your mortgage fast is that it costs you a tremendous amount of interest when you have a mortgage. Did you know that if you pay off your mortgage over 25 years at 12%, it will cost you about double the amount you borrowed in interest plus the original amount you borrowed? Shocking but true!

The accompanying chart shows that at 12% over 25 years, it costs $251,520 to borrow $120,000! Fortunately, interest rates are lower now, but we still pay huge amounts of interest when we take a mortgage.

Money Coach Rule

Buy your own home if at all possible. The joy of home ownership, the tax free position on sale, the traditionally good rate of return on real estate, plus the fact that it's an excellent form of forced saving all make home ownership a very attractive goal for just about anyone.

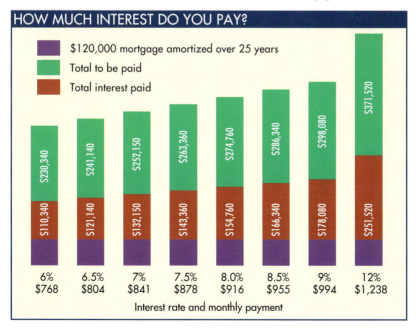

HOW MUCH INTEREST DO YOU PAY?

Legend:
- $120,000 mortgage amortized over 25 years
- Total to be paid
- Total interest paid

Interest rate and monthly payment	Total to be paid	Total interest paid
6% $768	$230,340	$110,340
6.5% $804	$241,140	$121,140
7% $841	$252,150	$132,150
7.5% $878	$263,360	$143,360
8.0% $916	$274,760	$154,760
8.5% $955	$286,340	$166,340
9% $994	$298,080	$178,080
12% $1,238	$371,520	$251,520

These are two major reasons why you should pay off that mortgage as soon as possible.

What's the difference between mortgage term and amortization period?

As an introduction to this topic of mortgages, it's important to distinguish between a mortgage "term" and the "amortization period."

The mortgage term is the length of time the mortgage agreement is in effect. The mortgage agreement outlines (among other things) the interest rate, the frequency of payment, the amount to be paid each week or month, the penalty clauses if any, various paydown options and the length of the term (usually 6 months, 1 year, 2 years, 3 years, or 5 years).

The amortization period is the length of time it will take the mortgage to be completely paid off. The shorter the amortization period, the sooner the mortgage will be paid off.

Let's say you borrow $50,000 to buy a home (i.e., you take a $50,000 mortgage), taking a term of 5 years at 8.25% with a 25-year amortization.

It would cost $390.00 per month for 5 years. At the end of that time, if interest rates remained the same and you continued to pay $390.00 per month, you would have 20 years left to pay off the debt. However, if interest rates had gone up, your payments would have to increase too.

It's vital to know though, using the example above, that at the end of the first 5-year term, you must not renew at a 25-year amortization, or you'll never pay the mortgage off! It must be renewed, in this example, at a 20-year amortization. Again, the shorter the period of amortization, the quicker the mortgage will be paid off.

To learn how to make your mortgage payments tax deductible, see page 73.

• COACH'S PLAYBOOK •

Four great ways to pay off your mortgage fast

Now, let's look at 4 ways to pay off your mortgage as quickly as possible.

1. Reduce the amortization period

Let's go back to the example we used earlier: A $50,000 mortgage at 8.25% costs $390.00 per month and amortized (paid off) in 25 years. Examine the chart on the left and note that over the 25-year life of the mortgage, the homeowner/borrower will pay a total of $116,884. Of that, $50,000 is the repayment of the principal, the rest is interest paid in after-tax dollars.

Now look at what happens if the borrower decides to take a 20-year amortization period. The monthly payments will increase by about only $30, but the debt will be paid off five years earlier, and he would have paid back $101,208 — a saving of over $15,000! If we really push to reduce the amortization period to 15 years, we pay $481 per month, or a total of $86,590 and save over $30,000 compared with the cost of a 25-year amortization.

When shopping for a mortgage, then, pay as much as you can afford monthly in order to obtain the shortest amortization period possible. You'll save thousands of dollars.

Slash your mortgage payments!

How reducing amortization period can cut your total mortgage payment by thousands of dollars.

	A	B	C
Mortgage amount	$50,000	$50,000	$50,000
Amortization	25 Years	20 Years	15 Years
Interest rate	8.25%	8.25%	8.25%
Monthly payment	389.61	421.70	481.06
Annual payment	4,675.32	5,060.40	5,772.72
Payment over the life of the mortgage	$116,884.32	$101,208.44	$86,589.93
B & C reduce their cost by		$15,675.88	$30,294.39

2. Make "double-up payments" whenever possible

The chart on page 82 shows the value of making two "extra" monthly payments a year, i.e., making 14 payments a year rather than 12.

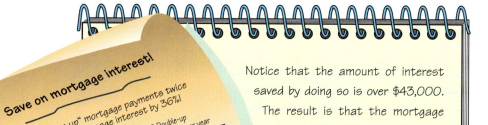

Save on mortgage interest!

How "doubling up" mortgage payments twice a year can cut mortgage interest by 36%!

	Regular Mortgage (25 years @8.25%)	2 Double-up payments per year
Mortgage principal	$90,000	$90,000
interest paid	$120,392	$77,140
interest saved		$43,252 (36%)
Years until mortgage paid off	25 years	17 years, 1 month

Notice that the amount of interest saved by doing so is over $43,000. The result is that the mortgage will be paid off almost 8 years earlier than would otherwise have been the case. In effect, the amortization period has been reduced, and thousands of dollars have been saved because the "double-up payments" serve to reduce the principal owing and therefore reduce the interest paid too.

3. Make weekly rather than monthly payments

The advantage here is similar to making double-up payments. By paying monthly, there are 12 cycles in the year. But by paying weekly, there are 13 cycles (i.e., 52 weeks÷4 = 13 cycles). This extra "cycle" really constitutes a "double-up payment" and has the effect of reducing the amortization period and therefore the amount of money actually paid.

4. Make lump sum payments

Many banks or trust companies that offer mortgages now allow the option of making a one time annual lump sum payment of 10% or even 15% of the original mortgage amount. If you borrowed $50,000 originally, you would be allowed to pay $5,000 (10%) or $7,500 (15%) against the principal amount annually — often on the anniversary date of the mortgage.

Again the effect is to reduce the amortization period and the total amount of interest you pay by thousands of dollars, and thus free your capital for other investments or important family or personal projects.

RRSP OR MORTGAGE PAYDOWN?

People often ask me whether they should contribute to their RRSP or pay down their mortgage.

The answer is yes—to both questions. Here's how I suggest they do it.

Make your maximum annual RRSP contribution if at all possible. One reason, of course, is to get a tax break, but the other factor is time. The longer your money is invested tax free, the larger the amount it will become. Don't wait to start your RRSP until you've paid off your mortgage— start now!

Then, take the tax savings you get from your RRSP contribution and use it to pay down your mortgage. If you contribute $6,000 to your RRSP and get a $2,500 tax return, put that against your mortgage. The rule of thumb is that by every dollar you reduce your mortgage, you save between $3 and $4 in interest payments over the life of your mortgage.

If you use this strategy every year, you can effectively build your RRSP and significantly reduce your mortgage at the same time.

LIFE INSURANCE: BUY TERM AND INVEST THE DIFFERENCE

It's probably fair to say that most people should have life insurance coverage equal to about five to 10 times their salary. Canadians average about three to four times their salary. Part of the reason is that we continue to buy a more expensive type of insurance than is necessary, and can't afford the right amount of coverage. This is a major problem, because life insurance is one of the most important purchases a family makes. It's therefore critical to make the right decision.

WHAT'S THE PURPOSE OF LIFE INSURANCE?

Life insurance is not really "life insurance" at all! It's probably better to call it income replacement insurance or financial protection for dependents. If you were to die tomorrow, your life insurance should replace your income for your dependents. But there's more to it than that!

HOW MUCH DO I NEED?

The answer probably is "more than you thought!" There are several things that insurance should do for your heirs:

" "

Coach's Quote

"Lack of money is the root of all evil." — Mark Twain

It should replace your income

We have a habit of living to the level of our income. If you earned $50,000 at the time of your death, you will ideally have provided the means by which your family could continue to enjoy a $50,000 income after your death. How do you do this?

The simple answer is to say that you require 10 times the level of your current income in life insurance to ensure this level, i.e., $50,000 income × 10 = $500,000 life insurance invested at 10% = $50,000. Of course, many people have term insurance coverage at work of up to three to five times their salary, and this should be a factor in deciding how much additional coverage is required. The truth is that while a 10% return is not impossible, the proceeds from a life insurance policy would probably be placed in a very conservative investment such as a GIC. So an 8% return may be more realistic. This means you would need $625,000 in coverage to ensure a $50,000 income in perpetuity for your heirs.

It should consider the surviving spouse's No. 1 enemy: inflation

An insurance policy that provides a $50,000 income in year #1 is great! But, several years later, that $50,000 is significantly reduced in terms of purchasing power. That may put tremendous pressure on a family, especially if it means that an untrained spouse is forced to return to the work force. Even then, it may not be enough to keep the family afloat.

It's true many people may be prepared to return to work after the death of a spouse. While this may reduce the amount of insurance required to replace income, a general rule of thumb is that one should consider life insurance coverage ranging between five and 10 times the current gross income!

Inflation's effect on reducing purchasing power is the flip side of the power of compounding on savings. It must be considered in determining how much insurance is required, and it may require the purchase of up to an additional $100,000 or more of life insurance.

It should pay off all debt

This includes your mortgage and any other debt you may have, including car loans, bank loans, etc. The last thing a grieving spouse needs at the time of death is to be burdened with debt of any kind. The implication here is that both spouses should be covered to a level that will pay off all debt.

It should cover future obligations

These obligations would probably include immediate funeral expenses up to $15,000, current day-care expenses (if applicable), and longer-term university or college expenses. While you probably expect (as I do) that the student should cover at least some expenses, a sum for assistance should be incorporated here.

THE THEORY OF DECREASING RESPONSIBILITY

One of the most common misunderstandings about life insurance is a belief that it is a permanent need of families. This is not true! Life insurance is a means of "buying time" until you get your financial house in order. You need more coverage when you're younger — less when you're older.

When your responsibilities are greatest, i.e., when you're young and have children and a mortgage, your insurance needs are greatest. As you age, your payments and mortgage are reduced until you reach the point of owning your home outright. This is the time when your death protection needs (in the form of insurance) are reduced and you can instead focus on accumulating cash for your retirement years.

YOUR INSURANCE NEEDS

Early in life you require more coverage...	Later in life you require less coverage...
1. Debts are many (eg., mortgage, car)	1. Few debts (eg., no mortgage)
2. Children are young	2. Children are grown
3. Loss of income would cause family suffering	3. Saving for retirement
Few assets Many obligations	Many assets Few obligations

For a discussion of the important role insurance can play in estate planning see page 113.

WHAT KIND OF INSURANCE SHOULD I BUY?

You should buy low-cost, convertible and renewable term insurance rather than more expensive whole life insurance and invest the difference between the cost of the two in a promising investment program. Specifically, I recommend you be the owner of one or more mutual funds either inside or outside an RRSP.

WHAT'S TERM INSURANCE?

Term insurance is a simple low cost insurance that has only one provision: If you die, your heirs will receive a stipulated amount of money. Period. In a sense, it's similar to home or car insurance. You want protection to a certain level for a certain period, as cheaply as you can get it! You'd laugh if someone suggested a savings or investment program should be part of your car or home insurance coverage.

WHAT'S WHOLE LIFE INSURANCE?

Whole life insurance offers a promise to pay a fixed amount (face value) on death combined with an investment or savings or "cash value" program. But when you die, your beneficiary receives only the face value; the cash value stays with the insurance company. Can you believe it? This combination of features is called the "bundling concept."

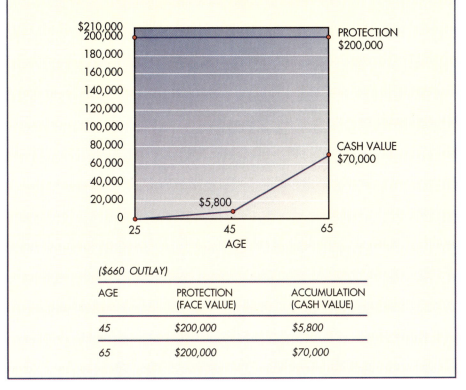

CHOICE #1: WHOLE LIFE INSURANCE "THE BUNDLING CONCEPT"

Bundling is the major flaw of whole life insurance. With this type of policy, you are required to buy your death benefit protection and your cash value benefit in one policy. By bundling your protection and your cash accumulation, you get minimum coverage on death (only $200,000) and inadequate cash for retirement if you live.

($660 OUTLAY)

AGE	PROTECTION (FACE VALUE)	ACCUMULATION (CASH VALUE)
45	$200,000	$5,800
65	$200,000	$70,000

Now let me suggest a much better option: Choice #2. Buy term and invest the difference in an RRSP!

CHOICE #2: BUY THE RIGHT KIND OF LIFE INSURANCE

Buy Term (age 25)

Whole Life	**Term**
(Guaranteed level Premium/	(Ten-year renewable term)
non-participating)	
$200,000 coverage	$200,000 coverage
Annual Premium $660	Initial Premium $236

... and invest the difference

Cash value after 20 years
(age 45) = **$5,800**
Cash value after 40 years
(age 65) = **$70,000**

Difference in annual premiums invested in a RRSP for

	20 years (age 45)	*40 years (age 65)*
at 5%	$5,874	($51,211)
at 6%	$7,351	($39,800)
at 10%	$15,580	$70,237
at 12%	$21,579	$205,858
at 15%	$34,007	$856,172

Which would you prefer?

Note: Rates for choices 1 & 2 are based on 1997 rates of a leading Canadian insurance company. Rates and benefits vary by company

INSURANCE REPLAY

Follow these rules/coaching tips for buying life insurance:

- Buy only low-cost term insurance. Compare the rates of several companies which offer term insurance and buy the least expensive policy you can find.

- Buy adequate coverage. While circumstances are different for everyone, a general rule of thumb is to hold coverage of between five and 10 times your current income.

- Compare the cost of term and whole life coverage — buy term and invest the difference. Be an owner and not a loaner, i.e., buy mutual funds — don't lend your money to a bank/trust company.

- Use insurance as an estate planning tool.

- Singles and children generally require only enough insurance to cover burial costs. Singles who don't have dependents don't require income replacement.

- Children generally don't require anything more than burial expenses.

- Stay away from fancy and costly insurance options. Don't "load up" with accidental death, option to purchase additional insurance, child riders, etc.

- Mortgage insurance is nothing more than life insurance. Don't have a separate mortgage insurance policy; rather, increase the level of life coverage on both spouses. The same is true of short-term debt, i.e., bank and car loans, etc. It tends to be much more expensive to insure these loans than to buy additional life insurance.

CHAPTER 5

ENRICH YOUR

RETIREMENT

wo sure-fire ways to achieve growth, tax relief, and security at retirement

Gone are the days when, at age 65 with the obligatory company watch in hand, the retiree finds his rocking chair, lights up the pipe, and withdraws from life.

Today's retiree is often younger, healthier, involved in a variety of sports or activities, and determined not to withdraw from life. Today's retiree also has plans to travel, perhaps extensively, and recognizes that his or her involvement and interests can be comparatively expensive.

They also recognize that they have one quarter to one third of their life ahead of them. In many cases, particularly if they have a solid pension, today's retirees will be in the same tax bracket as they were when they were earning a salary! For all those reasons, while security will be a higher priority than it was earlier, one cannot ignore the other objectives of growth and tax relief! You can't finance one quarter to one third of your life if inflation is devouring your purchasing power.

1. ROLL YOUR RETIREMENT GRATUITY/RETIRING ALLOWANCE INTO AN RRSP

Many people receive a lump sum payment called a "retirement gratuity" or "retiring allowance" at the time of retirement. This amount is eligible to be "rolled over" into an RRSP and under most circumstances should be.

If you do place it in a RRSP, you do not pay tax on it (which would be up to nearly 50% of the payment!), and it can continue to grow and compound tax free until you take it out. As we'll see in a moment, it can remain in your RRSP until you are 69.

Let's say you retire at 57, that you receive a retiring allowance of $40,000, and that you invest it and receive a 12% average annual return on the money. What will the $40,000 grow to by the time you turn 69? Well, the Rule of 72 tells us that at 12%, it would double in six years (72 ÷ 12 = 6). Therefore, it will grow to $80,000 when you're 63 (57 + 6), and to $160,000 by the time you turn 69 (63 + 6)!

You can be pretty conservative and still get 12%. Thus, by rolling over your retirement allowance into a conservative RRSP, you can still get growth (from $40,000 to $160,000), tax relief (you achieve tax-free growth within an RRSP), and security (through conservative investment).

2. LEAVE YOUR RRSPS IN PLACE AS LONG AS YOU CAN

It's important to leave your RRSPs as long as possible in order to allow the greatest amount of tax-free compounding that you can achieve and defer paying taxes as long as possible. Current rules allow you to continue to hold RRSPs until the year in which you turn 69.

To do this of course, the corollary is that you will live on pension income or other earned income. You may wish to continue to work part time or on a consulting basis. These activities will generate earned income and, ideally, will allow you to leave your RRSPs undisturbed for the longest possible time, i.e., until 69.

If it is not possible to leave your RRSPs untouched until age 69, it's comforting to know that if you hold your RRSPs in mutual funds, you can easily arrange a periodic withdrawal program that meets your needs. Note that this is not generally true with GICs, which are "locked in" for a predetermined period of time, and it's another reason why I recommend the flexibility of mutual funds. It's

Money Coach Rule

You simply cannot afford to ignore the importance of growth and tax relief as investment objectives even after you retire. If you do, it's at your peril!

important to remember that whenever you withdraw money from an RRSP, you pay tax on it, at your then-current marginal rate of tax.

A last quick word on inflation . . . it never retires! Historically, inflation has chewed away at our earning power at the rate of about 5% per year. Put another way, earnings must increase by at least 5% just to stay "even."

You may have just retired and have a current income of $40,000. You've likely got another 20 to 25 years to live. Look at the accompanying chart and note how much your annual income will have to be in 20 to 25 years just to keep up with inflation. I'll bet you're shocked at the figure!

INFLATION AT 5% MEANS TROUBLE

PRESENT INCOME	10 YEARS	15 YEARS	20 YEARS	25 YEARS
$20,000	$32,578	$41,579	$53,066	$67,727
$25,000	$40,722	$51,973	$66,332	$84,659
$30,000	$48,867	$62,368	$79,599	$101,591
$35,000	$57,011	$72,762	$92,865	$118,522
$40,000	$65,156	$83,157	$106,132	$135,454
$45,000	$73,300	$93,552	$119,398	$152,386
$50,000	$81,445	$103,946	$132,665	$169,318
$55,000	$89,589	$114,341	$145,931	$186,250
$60,000	$97,734	$124,736	$159,198	$203,181

The chart above shows how much your income must grow just to meet the effects of 5% inflation. For example, today's $60,000 must grow to $203,181 in 25 years just to stay even with the higher cost of living brought on by inflation.

Remember too, you'll likely be paying tax on all your income.

HERE'S HOW TO ACHIEVE GROWTH, TAX RELIEF, AND SECURITY AFTER AGE 69

Under current legislation, your RRSPs must be "collapsed" in the year in which you turn 69. What happens to your money then? Essentially you have five options:

1. Place your money in a Registered Retirement Income Fund (RRIF).

2. Buy a Life Income Fund (LIF).

3. Buy an annuity.

4. A combination of the three options outlined above.

5. Withdraw some or all of it and pay tax on it at that time. This option is not recommended unless income is required at that time.

   In this section we'll examine the alternatives and offer suggestions.

WHAT IS A RRIF?

A RRIF is the logical extension of an RRSP because only RRSP funds can be transferred into it. Note the RRSP focuses on savings (registered retirement *savings* plan) and the RRIF emphasizes income (registered retirement *income* fund). You have been saving for several years, and now it's time to receive income.

A RRIF is structured such that a minimum annual withdrawal is required, although a larger withdrawal may be made.

The following chart shows minimum RRIF payments per year. Notice that while the former rules required a RRIF balance of zero at age 90, a RRIF can now be held for life.

Note too that a RRIF can be purchased before age 69, but you must withdraw a minimum amount from a RRIF every year. Thus, because the withdrawn amount is taxed, it seems better under ideal conditions to delay purchase of a RRIF until it's necessary, i.e., age 69.

WHAT ARE THE ADVANTAGES OF A RRIF?

ADVANTAGE #1

All investments eligible for RRSPs are also eligible for RRIFs, so it's possible to continue to hold the same portfolio in your RRIF as you held in your RRSP if that's your wish. With a judicious mix of assets, it's still possible and indeed desirable to seek longer term growth within the RRIF, so that even though a minimum amount is withdrawn every year, the total income received may be dramatically greater than the original investment.

MINIMUM RRIF PAYMENT	
Age at the start of the year	%*
65	4.00
66	4.17
67	4.35
68	4.55
69	4.76
70	5.00
71	7.38
72	7.48
73	7.59
74	7.71
75	7.85
76	7.99
77	8.15
78	8.33
79	8.53
80	8.75
81	8.99
82	9.27
83	9.58
84	9.93
85	10.33
86	10.79
87	11.33
88	11.96
89	12.71
90	13.62
91	14.73
92	16.12
93	17.92
94	20.00
95	20.00
96	20.00
97	20.00
98	20.00
99	20.00
100	20.00

ADVANTAGE #2

RRIFs are designed to provide inflation protection through increased payments every year. You'll remember that we spoke earlier of the insidiousness of inflation and how it works to reduce our purchasing power continuously. Inflation will be with us throughout our lives, so the inflation protection provided by a RRIF is a real advantage.

HOW A RRIF FIGHTS INFLATION

Assume total RRIF value of $200,000

Minimum withdrawal

@ 71 $200,000 ¥ 7.38% = $14,760

@ 75 $200,000 ¥ 7.85% = $15,700

@ 85 $200,000 ¥ 10.33% = $20,660

@ 95 $200,000 ¥ 20.00% = $40,000

You can see from these figures how a RRIF ensures inflation protection by requiring an increased payout each year.

Money Coach Rule

RRIFs generally appear to do a better job of consistently achieving the goals of growth, tax relief, and security than an annuity. And that's why a RRIF is generally my choice.

ADVANTAGE #3

Note that these are minimum withdrawals. Should you want or need a larger amount, that can easily be arranged. This flexibility is another RRIF advantage.

ADVANTAGE #4

The assets are yours! Estate planning is a part of retirement planning and it's important to know that if you die before age 90, any remaining RRIF assets go either to your spouse or your estate. Your spouse can continue to receive the annual payments if named beneficiary. If your beneficiary is not your spouse, taxes must be deducted from the fund balance before it's paid to the estate. Like an RRSP it's certainly preferable to make a spouse the beneficiary of your RRIF. In either event, the fact that you own a RRIF ensures that you can provide for your beneficiaries.

It's clear then that a RRIF has many advantages.

WHAT IS A LIFE INCOME FUND (LIF)?

Until recently, retired Canadians who wanted to draw regular income from their locked-in pension money were required to buy an annuity soon after turning 69—there was no choice.

A LIF (which is now available in most provinces) represents an option whereby people with locked-in pensions can, if they wish, postpone buying an annuity until age 80 by purchasing a LIF.

One advantage of this new option is that a person is not forced to buy an annuity at age 69 when interest rates may be at unusually low levels. He or she can wait until interest rates rise and perhaps receive a higher level of income from the annuity, since annuity rates are closely connected to interest rates.

A second advantage is that, during the period between ages 69 and 80, the LIF can hold the same range of investments as a registered retirement income fund (RRIF) which may provide better growth, especially if interest rates are low during that particular period.

A third advantage is that if a person does select a guaranteed rate investment, it can be selected for a fixed period of time. At the end of that time the money is available for reinvestment (perhaps at a higher rate) for another period of time up to age 80. At that point an annuity must be purchased.

WHAT IS AN ANNUITY?

An annuity is simply a contract with an insurance company or other financial institution that promises you fixed, periodic payments for a set period in return for an initial lump-sum investment you make. When you buy an annuity you are essentially buying a stream of income.

Your investment decision is limited to the initial purchase, i.e., when to buy, what type to buy, and from whom to buy. Beyond that initial decision, you have little flexibility to change your mind or the nature of your assets.

Annuities can be purchased from insurance and trust companies. Generally, your income is determined at the time of purchase, depending on the level of interest rates in the market at that time and you are usually "locked in" to that rate. This, of course, is attractive if you buy at a time when rates are higher than normal, and much less attractive if you buy when rates are uncharacteristically low. As a general rule of thumb, you can buy a monthly income stream that is approximately 1% of the funds used to buy it, i.e., a $100,000 annuity offers approximately $1,000 per month.

BASIC TYPES OF ANNUITY

There are three basic types of annuity:

1. LIFE ANNUITY

A life annuity pays the highest annual income for life, but payments cease entirely upon your death. If there are any assets remaining at the time of your death, they are kept by the insurance or trust company. In theory, it's possible for one to purchase a $100,000 annuity, receive one $1,000 payment and then die. The remaining $99,000 would remain the property of the insurance or trust company. Under this plan there would be no provision for any of the money to go to one's spouse or family.

One way to avoid such an extreme situation is to purchase a life annuity with guaranteed term. The guaranteed term can be as short as five years or as long as the time until age 90.

Let's assume one purchased a plan like this with a 10-year guaranteed period and died in year six. The spouse or beneficiary would continue to receive payments for four more years. If at that time there are remaining assets, they remain the property of the insurance company or trust company. Note too that for every "extra" attached to this annuity, including the guaranteed period, the monthly income is reduced. (If you outlive the guaranteed period, you will continue to receive payments for the rest of your life — it is a life annuity.)

2. JOINT-AND-LAST-SURVIVOR LIFE ANNUITY

This type of annuity makes payments on the lives of two people, ensuring payments until the death of the last surviving spouse, and can be valuable in providing peace of mind that your spouse would be guaranteed a certain level of income even after your death.

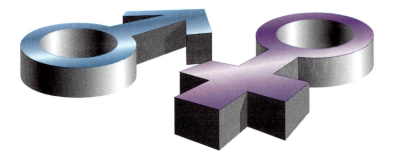

This annuity can also be bought with a guaranteed term, and it is possible to arrange lower payments to the survivor after the death of a spouse. These can be 25% or 50% lower on the assumption that it costs less for one to live than two.

Again, the "extras" built into the plan will affect the monthly income received. In the situation described above, when the survivor accepts a lower payment on the death of a spouse, there would be slightly higher income when both were alive. But even here, the estate would receive nothing following the death of the last surviving spouse unless there was a guaranteed period attached to the annuity and it had not expired.

3. FIXED-TERM ANNUITY

This type provides payments for a fixed period of time — specifically until you or your spouse reach age 90. There are no further payments regardless of how long you live.

However, this annuity allows for your estate to receive any remaining payments after the death of both spouses, if both deaths occur before age 90 — the end of the fixed term. The remaining money would be taxed as a total before being paid to the estate. In this respect, this annuity is different from the others mentioned above, which do not allow benefits to heirs; on the other hand, income ceases at age 90.

ANNUITIES IN SUMMARY

Overall, annuities tend to be less flexible than many people would like and certainly less flexible than a wisely selected RRIF.

When you purchase an annuity, you essentially turn your money over to an insurance or trust company, and you give up any future control over the funds. In return, you are promised an annual income. This income is usually fixed and therefore is eroded by inflation, although some annuities have now begun to introduce an inflation factor. When this is part of an annuity, a lower starting annual income almost invariably results.

A COMBINATION OF RRIFs AND ANNUITIES

Review the accompanying table, and select the options best suited to meet your needs. While I believe a RRIF most effectively meets the basic investment objectives of growth, tax relief, and security, it is true that for some people, certain aspects of an annuity may be particularly appealing. For example, for someone concerned about caring for a spouse until death regardless of age, a joint-and-last-survivor annuity may be appropriate.

These are critical decisions, and it's important to consult with your professional advisor who will be able to assist you in making the right decision and selecting the right option or options for you. Fortunately, it doesn't have to be either a RRIF or an annuity.

RETIREMENT INCOME OPTIONS

Here are the retirement options that provide growth, tax relief, and security.

	ANNUITIES			RRSPs	RRIFs
	LIFE ANNUITY	JOINT & LAST SURVIVOR	FIXED TERM		
GROWTH					
Growth potential	No	No	No	Yes	Yes
Compounding tax free	No	No	No	Yes	Yes
TAX RELIEF					
Minimizing taxes	Yes	Yes	Yes	Yes	Yes
SECURITY					
Payment flexibility	No*	No*	No*	Yes	Yes
Inflation protection	No*	No*	No*	Yes	Yes
Control over assets	No	No	No	Yes	Yes
Protection for spouse	No	Yes	Yes	Yes	Yes
Leaving an estate	No	No	Yes	Yes	Yes

*Some protection if you have indexed payments.

REVERSE MORTGAGE

Another option which is becoming increasingly popular with retired people is the reverse mortgage which allows people in retirement to use the equity which has been built up in their home over the years.

Here's how it works. A mortgage is taken out on the home. The owner has the option of taking up to about 35% of this mortgage money in cash, and the balance is used to buy an annuity. If a life annuity is selected, regular income will be received for life. If a joint-and-last survivor annuity is chosen, income will be received as long as one spouse remains alive. The income supplements any other source of retirement income which is being received.

When the owner or the last surviving spouse (if a joint annuity has been selected) dies, the house is sold and the principal as well as the interest which have been accruing over the years are repaid. Any remaining money goes to the estate.

On page 100 there is an example provided by Home Earnings Reverse Mortgage Corporation. In this case, the homeowner is 74 years old. The current value of the home is $250,000 and the mortgage available is $104,400 at an interest rate of 10.75% The owner has opted to take a lump sum payment of $4,400 with the remainder ($100,000) used to purchase a life annuity that generates a monthly income of $993.79 as long as she lives (even though our examples run only to age 90).

Notice in the example that at 5% annual growth in the value of the home, if the owner remains in the program to age 90 or beyond, the mortgage amount becomes greater than the value of the home. In this case, the insurance company would suffer a loss, not the homeowner or her estate.

A reverse mortgage has many attractive features. All the income received is essentially tax free. No payments are made against the mortgage and the title to the home remains with the homeowner.

There are a couple of cautions however. For one, it's probably not wise to take a reverse mortgage at too early an age. One reason is that the younger you are, the longer you will be expected to live with the result that the annuity payments will be lower than you may wish or need. Another reason is that the longer your life expectancy, the more unpaid interest will accumulate on your mortgage and the size of the mortgage available to you will be reduced.

The second caution is that you may not be entirely comfortable with the fact that you are carrying a significant debt at an older age. Many of us work hard to be relieved of debt and a reverse mortgage puts us back in that position. As well, depending on the importance of leaving a substantial estate, a reverse mortgage may not be best for you since the mortgage and accumulated interest will be paid to the mortgage company and not to your heirs or estate.

But if you are comfortable with the debt while you're living and feel that the equity built up in your home over the years should be yours to enjoy, a reverse mortgage may be an ideal means of increasing your income level to one which will allow you to enjoy your retirement years more fully.

		HOME VALUE INCREASING AT 5.00%			HOME VALUE INCREASING AT 7.00%		
Age	Annual Income	Amount Owing	Home Value	Equity in Home	Amount Owing	Home Value	Equity in Home
74	11,925	104,400	250,000	145,600	104,400	250,000	145,600
75	11,925	115,925	262,500	146,575	115,925	267,500	151,575
76	11,925	128,721	275,625	146,904	128,721	286,225	157,504
77	11,925	142,931	289,406	146,475	142,931	306,261	163,330
78	11,925	158,709	303,877	145,168	158,709	327,699	168,990
79	11,925	176,229	319,070	142,842	176,229	350,638	174,409
80	11,925	195,682	335,024	139,342	195,682	375,183	179,500
81	11,925	217,283	351,775	134,492	217,283	401,445	184,162
82	11,925	241,269	369,364	128,095	241,269	429,547	188,277
83	11,925	267,903	387,832	119,929	267,903	459,615	191,712
84	11,925	297,476	407,224	109,747	297,476	491,788	194,312
85	11,925	330,314	427,585	97,271	330,314	526,213	195,899
86	11,925	366,777	448,964	82,187	366,777	563,048	196,270
87	11,925	407,266	471,412	64,147	407,266	602,461	195,196
88	11,925	452,223	494,983	42,760	452,223	644,634	192,410
89	11,925	502,144	519,732	17,588	502,144	689,758	187,614
90	11,925	557,575	545,719	0	557,575	738,041	180,466

Source: Home Earnings Reverse Mortgage Corporation

CHAPTER 6

ESTATE PLANNING

state planning is a subject that many people still aren't very comfortable discussing or even thinking about. It's a topic easy to ignore and put off until another day. They just don't seem to be able to "get around to it".

Unfortunately, that's still the situation for about half of the population. Even amongst those who have a Will and therefore feel (incorrectly) that they've got things taken care of, a large proportion haven't reviewed and updated it within the last three years to bring it into alignment with new legislation or changed family circumstances.

There's also a widespread misconception that estate planning is only for the wealthy or for the elderly. In fact, if you have **any** assets to pass on, estate planning is necessary. It has almost nothing to do with wealth or age . . . it's something nearly everyone has a stake in.

Estate planning represents one of the best opportunities you will ever have to provide special gifts or benefits to those you love, not only after your death, but during your lifetime as well. You can make decisions that may have a huge positive impact on the lives of others. But without a plan, you can impose havoc, conflict, and hardship on people you love. *You can't take it with you; but you can determine how it will be left behind.*

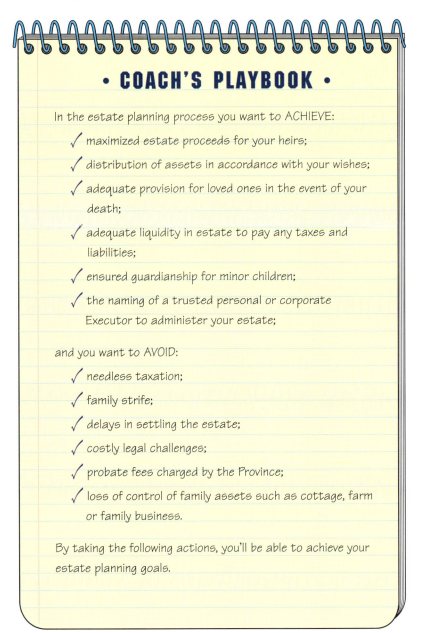

• COACH'S PLAYBOOK •

In the estate planning process you want to ACHIEVE:

✓ maximized estate proceeds for your heirs;

✓ distribution of assets in accordance with your wishes;

✓ adequate provision for loved ones in the event of your death;

✓ adequate liquidity in estate to pay any taxes and liabilities;

✓ ensured guardianship for minor children;

✓ the naming of a trusted personal or corporate Executor to administer your estate;

and you want to AVOID:

✓ needless taxation;

✓ family strife;

✓ delays in settling the estate;

✓ costly legal challenges;

✓ probate fees charged by the Province;

✓ loss of control of family assets such as cottage, farm or family business.

By taking the following actions, you'll be able to achieve your estate planning goals.

PREPARE A VALID, UP-TO-DATE WILL

This is the foundation of any estate plan and it includes many aspects.

WHAT IS A WILL?

- It is a legal document, signed in accordance with specific rules, that's designed to be your final statement of wishes. Properly designed and worded, your Will can ensure that your wishes are carried out with a minimum of expense or delay.

- It should be reviewed every 3 years or so to ensure it has not been affected by changes in legislation or family circumstance.

- It is implemented only on your death and remains private until that time.

- You may change or revoke the terms of your Will any time until your death as long as you are mentally competent to do so.

WHY IS A WILL IMPORTANT?

If you die without one, a number of negative things can happen including these:

- The beneficiaries of your estate may be determined by provincial law.

    This is a huge consideration! I constantly meet mature successful adults with a spouse, children, a home, a cottage and assets of a substantial value who haven't been able to find the time to have a Will drawn up. If they truly understood the consequences of dying without a Will they'd make a "beeline" to have one drawn up.

- The court may appoint an administrator for your estate and that person may not be the person you would have chosen. While it's often a spouse or family member who is chosen, it's still possible that you wouldn't have chosen that person. The court's choice can also lead to family strife and possible extra legal costs if a challenge is undertaken.

- Without a Will, distribution to heirs can be delayed for a significant period of time since no one can act until an administrator has been appointed by the court. This too can cause strife and added legal expenses.

- The court may appoint a guardian for minor children and the guardian may not be your choice. Surely, you know the perfect guardian for minor children … probably a relative or family friend. Can you be certain the court would choose that same person? Clearly not.

● The estate may be subject to needless taxation if it has not been properly arranged. Huge bites can be taken by both federal and provincial governments, whereas with a plan in place thousands of dollars in tax can be deferred or avoided.

• COACH'S PLAYBOOK •

IF YOU DIE WITHOUT A WILL, YOUR ESTATE IS
DISTRIBUTED AS FOLLOWS WHEN YOU LEAVE:

A Spouse and No Children or Grandchildren:

Everything goes to your spouse.

A Spouse and Child:

The first $200,000 plus 1/2 of the balance goes to your spouse. If the child is a minor, the Official Guardian will administer the funds. (Surely, you'd rather select the person to administer these funds, wouldn't you?)

A Spouse and Two or More Children:

The first $200,000, plus 1/3 of the remainder goes to your spouse. The remaining 2/3 will be shared equally by your children. The Official Guardian may be involved as above.

A Spouse and Parent (No Brother or Sister):

All to spouse.

A Spouse and Brother(s) or Sister(s):

All to spouse.

Spouse, Parent, and Brother(s) or Sister(s):

All to spouse.

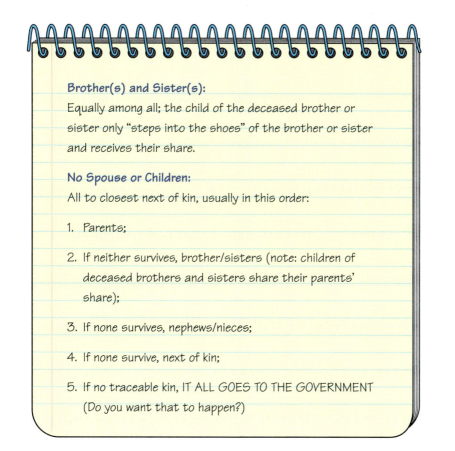

Brother(s) and Sister(s):
Equally among all; the child of the deceased brother or sister only "steps into the shoes" of the brother or sister and receives their share.

No Spouse or Children:
All to closest next of kin, usually in this order:

1. Parents;

2. If neither survives, brother/sisters (note: children of deceased brothers and sisters share their parents' share);

3. If none survives, nephews/nieces;

4. If none survive, next of kin;

5. If no traceable kin, IT ALL GOES TO THE GOVERNMENT (Do you want that to happen?)

WHAT TYPES OF WILLS ARE THERE?

A "holograph" Will is written in your handwriting and signed by you; no witness is necessary. A holograph Will is **NOT** recommended since your words may not clearly express your interests and lead to controversy as to your actual wishes.

A 'formal' Will is typed and signed by you in front of two witnesses (who may not be one of your beneficiaries or their spouse). It is usually drafted by a lawyer so as to ensure clear and precise intent.

> **Coach's Quote**
> Very few good things happen when one dies without a Will.

EXECUTOR SELECTION CHECK LIST

Here's a list of items to be considered when choosing your Executor:

	YES	NO
1. Can they act fairly and impartially towards all beneficiaries?	○	○
2. Are they geographically accessible?	○	○
3. Can they take time from their own jobs to devote to this task?	○	○
4. Could they work well with Co-Executors you may appoint?	○	○
5. Will they likely outlive you?	○	○
6. Are they aware of the personal liability they assume in case of errors they may make in carrying out the task?	○	○
7. Are they knowledgeable in the areas of:		
estate and trust laws?	○	○
taxation of estates and trusts?	○	○
insurance?	○	○
real estate?	○	○
investments?	○	○
8. If not knowledgeable in these areas, are they prepared to invest the time to become knowledgeable or to find experts to assist?	○	○
9. Do they have and can they maintain a good personal relationship with the family?	○	○
10. Are they prepared for and can they handle the potential criticism and challenges that may come from the family?	○	○
11. Have they agreed to act as Executor?	○	○

If the answers to these questions are predominately 'NO', you may want to look at other options or to involve a professional to assist your appointee.

Money Coach Rule

The Will truly is the foundation of any estate plan, and there is very little excuse for a mature individual, especially one who cares about his or her family, not to have one in place. The modest cost of $150 to $250 is more than offset by the peace of mind which it offers, and the knowledge that you have provided a structure which your Executor can use to ensure that your loved ones are cared for as you would want them to be.

HAVING A CONTINUING OR "ENDURING" POWER OF ATTORNEY

Continuing Power Of Attorney

The Substitute Decisions Act came into effect in Ontario in 1995. Under the provisions of this Act, a medical practitioner is required to notify the Office of the Public Trustee if you, your spouse or any adult children (i.e., 18 or over) are deemed incompetent to manage their financial affairs for any medical reason. In this situation, the Public Trustee would have complete management control of all your financial assets. Now how's that for scary?

Coach's Quote

In a word, the Power of Attorney is probably one of the most important documents you will ever sign, and everyone 18 or over in Ontario should have one.

The way to protect yourself and your family from this very harsh legislation is to ensure that you have a Continuing Power of Attorney. The contents of this document are specifically designed to be exercised during any subsequent legal incapacity and it complies fully with the **Powers of Attorney Act**.

So let's have a closer look at this important item.

WHAT IS A POWER OF ATTORNEY FOR FINANCIAL AFFAIRS?

It's a document given in writing by the donor (you) to another person (the attorney ... not to be confused with 'lawyer') to act on your behalf in conducting your financial affairs. It does not extend to decisions regarding medical treatment (see page 109). When you give someone this Power of Attorney, they can immediately sign documents on your behalf if you can't, either because you are away and unavailable or because you are ill. Because of the broad range of the power given, it's obviously important to select this person wisely. Note that all Powers of Attorney terminate in the event the person you appoint dies, or in the event of your death. You can revoke a Power of Attorney at any time if you are mentally competent.

A normal Power of Attorney is a legal document that gives one or more people the authority to manage your financial affairs. It can be "general", covering all aspects of your financial affairs or it can be "limited" to specific aspects. It would be valid only as long as you were mentally competent.

A "Continuing" or "Enduring" Power of Attorney will continue to be valid **even in the event of your incapacitation**, which is probably the condition under which it would be most useful. Creation of a Continuing Power can ensure that ongoing decisions can be made which are in your best interests. For this reason a spouse is normally given such authority.

YOU NEED BOTH POWER OF ATTORNEY AND A WILL

It's important to have both a Continuing Power of Attorney and a Will. You see, with a Power of Attorney, you give that person the power to act while you are alive, but unable to act for yourself. The Power of Attorney is terminated on your death. At this point, the Will takes effect and the Executor/Executrix named in your Will has authority to act.

Therefore, be aware that the person appointed as your Executor has **no authority or power** to act for you while you are alive. Even if you are legally incapacitated, the Executor cannot act. Only your Attorney, appointed through a Continuing Power of Attorney has the power to act while you are alive but unable to act for yourself.

It's for these reasons that we need **both** a Will and the Continuing Power of Attorney.

WHY IS A CONTINUING POWER OF ATTORNEY USEFUL?

There are many useful applications of a Continuing Power of Attorney including these:

- Not only can the person appointed act on your behalf immediately upon the documents being signed, they would also be able to act for you **even if** you were to become incapacitated. The power you grant "continues" and "endures" beyond your incapacitation and is therefore referred to as either a Continuing or Enduring Power of Attorney.

- Remember that a **normal** Power of Attorney is valid only as long as you are mentally competent. The real advantage of the Enduring Power of Attorney is its enduring nature, which makes it useful at just the times (i.e., mental incompetency due to accident or disease), when a normal Power of Attorney becomes invalid.

● If you are a business person, the Continuing Power of Attorney enables you to appoint someone to look after your business affairs if you are unable to because of accident or sickness.

● In Ontario, in order to sell or refinance the matrimonial home, the law requires the signature of both spouses on the Deed or Mortgage even though it may be registered in one spouse's name alone. Therefore, if one spouse is incapacitated and without the Continuing Power of Attorney, the second spouse is handcuffed. With it, such sale or refinancing could be undertaken.

● It is an invaluable tool in protecting yourself and your family against the possibility of the Office of the Public Trustee taking **complete** management control of **all** your financial affairs.

HAVE A POWER OF ATTORNEY FOR PERSONAL CARE AND A LIVING WILL

With the introduction of Ontario's new Substitute Decisions Act in 1995, a Power of Attorney for Personal Care became a legal document.

A Power of Attorney for Personal Care (defined as health care, nutrition, shelter, clothing, hygiene or safety) allows everyone 16 years of age and over (not 18 as in the Continuing Power of Attorney for Property) to name the person to make their personal care decisions if they are incapable of doing so. This includes the giving or withholding of consent to medical treatment.

Probably not everyone will attempt to list specific health care procedures to be administered or withheld in their Power of Attorney for Personal Care. Instead, they'll probably discuss their wishes with their attorney, and then write a statement in their

Money Coach Rule

For many of the same reasons outlined earlier regarding a Continuing Power of Attorney for Property, it's important that you have a Living Will and a Power of Attorney for Personal Care in place as soon as possible. By taking such actions now, you'll significantly increase the likelihood of your being able to die with dignity.

Power of Attorney for Personal Care that medical treatment should be discontinued if there's no reasonable expectation of recovering from life-threatening diseases. This statement is called a "Living Will". However, the Personal Care Attorney will have the final say.

Personal Care Attorneys who act in "good faith" are protected from any actions for damages and doctors who honor their decisions will also be protected by the new Consent to Treatment Act.

AVOID UNNECESSARY PROBATE FEES

What Is Probate?

Probate is a legal process that confirms a Will. Usually the Executor and/or your lawyer files for probate with the provincial court. Once processed, the court issues a Certificate of Appointment of Estate Trustee which confirms the validity of the Will. Financial institutions will not normally release assets of an estate to an Executor until they receive proof of such a Certificate (most of us still refer to this Certificate as Probate).

PROBATE FEES ACROSS THE COUNTRY	
British Columbia	Fee of $4 per $1,000 for the first $25,000; $6 per $1,000 thereafter (no maximum).
Alberta	Progressive rates starting at $25 for the first $10,000 increasing to a maximum of $6,000 for estates in excess of $1,000,000.
Saskatchewan	Up to $1,000, a flat fee of $6. For amounts above this limit, $12 for the first $1,000 and $6 per $1,000 thereafter (no maximum).
Manitoba	$5 per $1,000 (no maximum).
Ontario	$5 per $1,000 for the first $50,000 and $15 per $1,000 thereafter (no maximum).
Quebec	Probate not required for notarial wills; flat fee of $45 for English form wills.
New Brunswick	$5 per $1,000 (no maximum).
Newfoundland	Flat fee of $50 for the first $1,000; $4 per $1,000 thereafter (no maximum).
Nova Scotia	Progressive rates starting at $75 for the first $10,000, increasing to $500 for estates of $200,000 and $3 per $1,000 thereafter (no maximum).
Prince Edward Island	Progressive rates starting at $50 for the first $10,000, increasing to $400 for estates of $400,000 and $4 per $1,000 thereafter (no maximum).

Probate fees are payable to the court (the government) and are paid from the proceeds of the estate. Ontario probate fees are currently $5 per $1,000 for the first $50,000 and $15 per $1,000 thereafter with no maximum — virtually the highest in the country.

ESTIMATING PROBATE FEES

Canadian Assets	Current Value (Pre-tax)	Beneficiary Designation*		Joint Ownership with right of Survivorship*		Value of Estate for Probate
Registered	___	YES	NO	YES	NO	___
RRSP/RRIF proceeds	___	___	___	N/A	N/A	___
RPP lump sums & death benefit	___	___	___	N/A	N/A	___
Non-Registered Guaranteed Income Annuities	___	___	___	N/A	N/A	___
Other Income Securities	___	N/A	N/A	___	___	___
Growth Securities	___	N/A	N/A	___	___	___
Real Estate (Net of Debt)						
Principal Residence	___	N/A	N/A	___	___	___
Vacation Properties	___	N/A	N/A	___	___	___
Farm Properties	___	N/A	N/A	___	___	___
Land for Personal Use	___	N/A	N/A	___	___	___
Other	___	___	___	___	___	___
Total	___	___	___	___	___	___
Estimate of Probate Fees	___	___	___	___	___	___

(Refer to provincial rates and calculate potential fees based on total "Value of Estate for Probate")
* Generally, if answer is Yes in either of these categories, you may exclude value of asset for probate fee estimates

HOW CAN PROBATE FEES BE REDUCED?

a) Make your spouse your RRSP/RRIF beneficiary. This will make it possible for the funds in your plan(s) to pass directly to your spouse without tax and without becoming part of your estate and therefore without incurring probate costs.

b) Name an adult person, rather than your estate, as beneficiary of your life insurance policies and annuity contracts. This strategy precludes these assets becoming part of your estate and therefore avoids probate costs.

c) Hold non RRSP/RRIF assets as joint tenants. These assets include your home, cottage, other property, bank accounts, mutual funds, stocks, bonds and other assets. By doing so, the assets automatically pass to the surviving owner if one dies, without going into the estate and therefore without probate fees being charged.

d) Convert personal debt to corporate debt. Most personal debt is not a deduction for the purpose of determining a person's probateable estate. Therefore, it may be wise to move assets which have debt attached to them to a corporation, so that a deduction can effectively be taken on the debt. The asset that would fall into the estate for probate purposes would then be the shares of the company, not the investment portfolio. In valuing the company shares, all debts of the corporation would be included.

e) Create a private holding company in a low probate province. This approach to reducing probate is somewhat complicated and would be practical only if the estate were of substantial size. The mechanics would be to transfer the assets of an estate to a holding company established in a province with comparatively low probate fees such as Alberta. Multiple Wills would be required with a separate one to deal with the Alberta assets. The shares of the holding company would be subject to probate in Alberta, but currently their probate fees are limited to $6,000. In Ontario, a million dollar estate would generate probate fees of about $14,500.

f) Set up a living (or "inter vivos") trust. Assets held in a trust do not pass to your estate after death. A trust can be an effective estate planning device that is very flexible and can, for example, allow you to access its capital or income during your life. On death, assets pass to your intended beneficiaries according to the trust document — not the Will. **The result: no probate fees**.

A NOTE OF CAUTION

These options are intended to reduce probate fees, but the area of estate planning is quite complex. Some of the techniques described may impact on other aspects of the process including other potential tax liabilities and family law. To be sure, discuss the overall plan with your financial advisor who may wish to take legal or accounting counsel as well.

CONSIDER LIFE INSURANCE

While we usually consider the primary purpose of life insurance as replacing the income of the insured in case of death, it can have other importance as part of a well developed estate plan.

In this context, appropriate levels of life insurance can provide liquidity within an estate to pay off liabilities such as taxes, probate fees or mortgages and thus protect more of the estate's assets for its beneficiaries. It can also be used to ensure that in settling the estate, less liquid assets such as real estate might not need to be sold under duress and at a less than attractive price.

AN EXAMPLE:

Perhaps the best example of how life insurance can be used as an estate planning tool is in a situation like this:

On the death of your father, all his assets were passed on to your mother as part of a spousal rollover and no taxes were payable at the time.

Now however, your mother has passed away and on the day of her death, all of her capital assets were deemed to have been disposed of at fair market value. Capital assets are those which attract capital gains for tax purposes. Note that the assets were not sold; they were **deemed to have been disposed of**, at fair market value.

One major asset held by your mother, a large and valuable piece of land, had been in the family for years and had grown substantially in value. As part of Revenue Canada's calculations, the taxes owed by your mother's estate when this property was deemed to have been disposed of for tax purposes, was $100,000.

Without insurance coverage, it's quite possible that if there were not other assets in her estate that could be sold to pay the tax, the land itself may have to be sold. And given the sad condition of the real estate market over the last few years, it's quite possible that its sale might not even cover the tax liability.

Fortunately, your mother had good advice from her financial advisor, had calculated the taxes due on her passing, and had purchased $100,000 of term life or universal life* insurance to cover the liability. There is therefore no need to sell any of the estate's assets and thus diminish its size. By planning ahead, the beneficiaries of the estate will be in a much improved position. The one caveat in this strategy of course is that the person seeking to use life insurance as an estate planning tool must be insurable.

* (In some cases, universal life can be more effective than term to 100. Each case must be examined separately.)

Money Coach Rule

And as a final twist on the idea, how about this?

What about discussing this strategy with your children who may be beneficiaries of your estate, and suggest that they consider paying your annual insurance premium? You have created the means by which part of their inheritance can be protected from Revenue Canada, and yet you incur no extra costs in doing so if your beneficiaries pay the annual premium.

Benefits paid from life insurance are generally non-taxable regardless of whether they are left to a named beneficiary or to the estate. However, if left to the estate, they are subject to probate fees, so a named beneficiary is the most cost-effective.

An increasingly popular product available for estate planning purposes is called **Universal Life**. This product is a form of permanent life insurance which, when utilized properly, is an extremely effective way of ensuring that your assets end up in the hands of your heirs, while ensuring that Revenue Canada gets paid its taxes.

The key to this strategy is that it can be accomplished at a cost that amounts to mere pennies on the dollar.

Universal Life has a number of estate planning advantages including the fact that accumulated growth within the policy is tax free, and that investments can include a wide variety of options such as guaranteed investments, bond indexes, and equity indexes.

It's worth discussing the benefits of Universal Life with your financial advisor.

CONSIDER THE USE OF TRUSTS

WHAT IS A TRUST?

The concept of a trust goes back to about the Middle Ages. They were first used widely during the period of the Crusades, when individuals were away from home for prolonged periods. At such a time, it was important to create the means by which business and personal decisions could be carried out on one's behalf by someone else.

Simply stated, a trust involves the holding of trust property by one person for the benefit of another.

To create a valid trust, there must be a settlor, a trustee, and identifiable beneficiaries. Not all 3 parties must be different; for example, one person could be the settlor and also be a trustee. This could happen if parents were to create a trust during their lifetime for a child who was a dependant. A settlor could also be one of several trustees; but it is not legal to have a situation where the settlor is also the trustee and the sole beneficiary.

A trust can come into existence when legal title to some property has been transferred to a trustee, and although the trustee has legal title to the trust property, beneficial ownership rests with the beneficiaries.

Many types of assets can be put into a trust including bank accounts, shares of private businesses, stocks, bonds, mutual funds, and real estate.

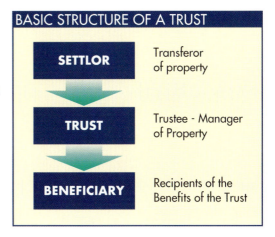

BASIC STRUCTURE OF A TRUST

SETTLOR — Transferor of property

TRUST — Trustee - Manager of Property

BENEFICIARY — Recipients of the Benefits of the Trust

TYPES OF TRUSTS

There are many different types and uses of trusts, but we're going to introduce only the main types; we're not dealing here with "corporate trusts" and only in passing with "offshore trusts" because they can become very complex and have convoluted tax and legal implications.

The two main types of trusts are **"living trusts"** and **"testamentary trusts"**.

Living Trusts (Sometimes also called Inter Vivos or Family Trusts)

A living trust, not surprisingly, is created while an individual is alive and comes into operation once the trust agreement is signed and the trust is funded.

A living trust may continue to exist after the settlor dies, or there may be provisions within the trust agreement whereby the trustee is given directions to terminate or collapse the trust and distribute the assets to the beneficiaries on the settlor's death.

A classic use to which a living trust is put is to transfer beneficial ownership of an asset to an intended beneficiary while still maintaining control over the asset. It would allow you, for example, to provide income from a trust to a spouse or child, while retaining control of the capital. It may apply where shares of a family business are placed in trust and yet the settlor wishes to continue to have influence in the business.

Living trusts can be designed as either **"revocable"** or **"irrevocable"**. Revocable living trusts allow the settlor to change his/her mind and reclaim some or all of the assets within the trust. However, the Income Tax Act severely curtails the tax advantages of revocable living trusts, and since the tax advantages are usually important considerations in establishing the trust in the first place, most living trusts are irrevocable. It's the permanent legal change in ownership that creates the tax advantages and estate planning opportunities of living trusts.

Testamentary Trusts

A testamentary trust takes effect upon your death, and the items establishing and providing for its operation are included in your Will. Testamentary trusts are funded out of the proceeds of the deceased's estate. Prior to one's death, we can modify the terms of the trust or even remove it, simply by having a new Will created. Because it's not technically established until one's death, its terms can be kept as private as your Will. And of course, by their nature, testamentary trusts are irrevocable.

Discretionary/Non-Discretionary

Both living and testamentary trusts can be established as **"discretionary"** or **"non-discretionary"**. A discretionary trust allows the trustee to use guidelines or to use discretion in determining the income to be paid to a beneficiary. For example, the trustee(s) may decide to use capital of the trust to allow a student beneficiary to pay tuition and expenses for university, medical or graduate school, even though it may erode the original capital of the trust. If in the trustees' mind, the primary intent of the trust was to fund such expenses rather than to retain the full original capital, they may use their discretion to make such payments, prior to the date of intended distribution. A non-discretionary trust does not contain documentary provision for trustee(s) to use discretion prior to the date of intended distribution.

Testamentary trusts can also be used to allow the testator to identify the purpose for which funds can be spent and may include educational costs, the purchase of a first home or nearly any other identified purpose. This approach is effective when the testator is unsure of how the funds might be spent if given without stated intent to a beneficiary not mature enough to make decisions on his or her own behalf.

Trusts are often useful to people in a second marriage who have children from a previous marriage. A trust can be set up so that the second spouse receives income for life from the trust assets. Following the second spouse's death, the remaining trust assets can be diverted to the children from the first marriage. Without a trust, assets could pass to the second spouse's beneficiaries.

• COACH'S PLAYBOOK •

DIFFERENCES BETWEEN LIVING AND TESTAMENTARY TRUSTS

Item	Living	Testamentary
Creation	Created during person's lifetime and begins to operate when funded.	Created by Will and begins to operate on death of individual.
Assets Into Trust	Assets transferred from settlor's name to trustee's name.	Assets flow to trust from deceased's estate.
Trustee(s)	Anyone including settlor.	Anyone (obviously excluding settlor; now deceased), and often the deceased's Executor.
Discretionary/ Non- Discretionary	May be either.	May be either.

TRUSTS AND TAXES

As trusts have evolved from their origins during the Medieval Period, they have come to be associated with tax planning to a greater and greater degree. And while there have been certain critical tax advantages in the past, tax changes over the last several years have stripped trusts of much of their tax attractiveness. This is by no means to suggest that they have no further tax advantages, but rather that they should be considered for **tax reasons AND estate planning reasons today**.

OFFSHORE TRUSTS

Much interest has been generated in recent years by offshore trusts. As our national debt mounts, as our taxes continue to soar, and as our winters seem to stretch on endlessly, Canadians have turned their attention to the attractiveness of offshore trusts. Particularly appealing are those in warm places like Bermuda, the Cayman Islands and the Turks and Caicos, although there are many parts of the world where offshore trusts can be created.

These structures have, as their primary purpose, the shielding of wealth from taxes, legally. As the name suggests, these offshore trusts are generally established outside the place of residence of either the beneficiaries or the settlor, i.e., the person who established the trust. The trustee is also a non-resident, and usually a corporation. As in any other trust, the assets in the trust become the legal property of the trustee, who holds the assets for the benefit of the beneficiaries.

IS AN OFFSHORE TRUST FOR YOU?

Money Coach Rule

One other point to consider regarding offshore trusts is that in order to set up a cost-effective offshore trust, you'll probably need a minimum of $250,000 Canadian. Offshore trusts, while they may apply in some cases, seem simply inappropriate in most situations.

There are probably only a few situations in which an offshore trust may be seriously considered:

1. You're planning to become a non-resident of Canada.

If you are moving overseas, an offshore trust may offer advantages. In this situation, the timing of the creation of the trust can be critical.

It's also important to recognize that the strict legal interpretation of the term "non-resident" will apply. It essentially means you're going to sever your ties with Canada, and this may involve practical considerations including the need to give up your OHIP card and your driver's license.

2. **You're a Canadian resident, but your beneficiaries are not.**

You may be an older Canadian in a high tax bracket who has children or grandchildren living overseas. In this case, income from the trust will be received by the beneficiaries of the trust (your children or grandchildren) and be taxed according to the tax laws in the country where they live. While many countries have lower tax rates than Canada, not all do.

3. **You're a non-resident of Canada with relatives here.**

Usually the person establishing the trust will be the one who has left the country permanently. The beneficiaries may be children or grandchildren living in Canada who will probably have to pay tax only on the income they receive from the trust.

PREPLAN FUNERAL ARRANGEMENTS

A prearranged funeral is a funeral arrangement made prior to death. It's a practical way of identifying your wishes for your own funeral, or for the funeral of someone for whom you are responsible.

WHAT ARE THE ADVANTAGES?

A prearranged funeral is part of a sensible estate plan. When you discuss a prearranged funeral with a funeral director, you have an opportunity to ask questions and to be sure you fully understand what services are provided and at what cost. You can make unhurried decisions regarding the type of service you wish, the type of casket you desire, and your preferences for burial, entombment or cremation. Such planning will serve as a helpful guide for family and friends and just seems to make practical sense.

WHY PREARRANGE A FUNERAL?

Planning for a funeral now will save others that responsibility later. Providing guidelines can only make things easier at a time of emotion and stress.

A number of nursing homes now require that funeral arrangements be in place before a resident enters a home. Also, health care professionals often recommend that families caring for terminally ill individuals make funeral arrangements.

It's also important to remember that while the funeral is for the person who has died, it also allows the survivors to satisfy their own emotional and psychological needs. For this reason, preplanning can allow room for the wishes of the family as to how the funeral should be conducted. So discussion with family, friends, clergy, and Executor is an important part of funeral pre-arrangement.

PREPLANNING MAKES SENSE

FOR YOU	FOR THE FAMILY
You select what you desire.	They know it's what you wanted.
You decide in the comfort of your home.	They'll have more time for family and friends.
You aren't rushed.	They won't need to make any hasty decisions.
You can save money.	They won't be financially burdened.
You enjoy peace of mind.	They will thank you.

ESTATE PLANNING CHECKLIST

(Check your estate planning progress as you accomplish each step.)

ITEM	DONE
1. I have prepared a valid up-to-date Will.	○
2. I have a Continuing Power of Attorney.	○
3. I have a Power of Attorney for Personal Care.	○
4. I have prepared a Living Will.	○
5. I have assured that my estate will not be subjected to unnecessary probate fees.	○
6. I have a record of personal affairs.	○
7. I have registered property jointly (where appropriate).	○
8. I have reviewed the consideration of life insurance.	○
9. I have reviewed the consideration of trusts.	○
10. I have assured that my estate will not be subjected to any unnecessary tax.	○
11. I have given gifts to family members (where possible).	○
12. I have preplanned all funeral arrangements.	○
13. I have given to charity on a preplanned basis.	○

CHAPTER 7

f you wish to build financial freedom for you and your family, it's essential to begin the task as soon as possible. The principles I've outlined so far will put you on the right track. If you stick with them over the long term, you are virtually assured of outstanding success.

The sooner you apply them, the sooner and more effectively you'll be ensuring financial independence not only for yourself but also for future generations of your family!

Here's an example of how time and consistency along with the "magic" of compounding can ensure financial freedom for generations to come:

Let's assume you start with nothing — which is probably as true for you as it was for me.

Coach's Quote

"Whether you think you can do it or not, you're right." — Henry Ford

You begin by saving $100 per month — more would be better, of course. In 20 years at a compound rate of 12%, you would have $91,121.

Now, let's say you wish to send your two children to university for a total of eight years, so you withdraw $10,000 per year ($5,000 every six months) for a total withdrawal of $80,000. Your original $91,121 minus the $80,000 would actually have grown to $91,714 (let's hear it for compounding!).

Now let's go even further and assume that you save $100 per month for 30 more years. Your $91,714 would grow to over $3,000,000!

Your children and their children of course continue to save $100 a month and for generations, your family will be able to use the investment that you started for education, housing, travel, emergencies, etc., and still pass it on to the next generations.

But as always, it's important to start now. As a friend of mine commented, "I should have started doing this stuff 20 years ago." I agreed. The best time to start was 20 years ago. The second best time to start is now!

Don't be discouraged by lost opportunities; focus on creating new opportunities for you, for your children, and for your children's children.

Your altitude is determined by your attitude — attitude is everything!

"I DON'T HAVE ANY MONEY"

There are books full of excuses for not acting: "The timing's not quite right." "I don't have any money." "I'm too busy right now." "I could never force myself to do that!"

All the education and knowledge available about how to become financially independent means absolutely nothing if you don't use that knowledge by applying it. It takes only a decision, commitment, and a few dollars to start you on your way. Remember, it doesn't take a fortune to make a fortune; all it takes is some time.

But, the sad truth is that most people will not act because they simply don't believe it can work for them. They've conditioned themselves to accept being average and ordinary, to accept financial difficulty, to accept being poor, and to accept being unhappy.

Fortunately, as I speak in different cities, I'm seeing growing numbers of people who view themselves differently — they see themselves as winners. They think and act like winners, and they become winners. They're the people who can stay motivated and stick to their plan to achieve financial independence for as long as it takes to happen.

"THE TIMING'S NOT QUITE RIGHT"

I'm noticing too that these often tend to be people who have their version of a money coach to work with and who helps them stay on course. Most definitely, there is a price to pay and priorities to be established and adhered to.

"I DON'T REALLY NEED SECURITY"

But I don't know anybody who has achieved financial independence who doesn't look back and say: "Yes, there was a price to pay but believe me, it was worth it!" Several of these people have told me too that if they had known how fantastic it would feel to be financially independent, they would have been willing to pay a much bigger price than they actually did.

Remember, a winning, healthy, positive attitude is not with us at birth. It is not the result of an injection or a pill, it is not part of a university degree program, and it is definitely not for sale. It's much simpler than that! (I've said all along the great truths are the simplest!) It's the result of a simple decision that you have the ability to make. A decision to be extraordinary rather than ordinary, happy rather than sad, positive rather than negative, wealthy rather than poor — in short, a decision to be a winner in all areas of life.

Remember the goal? It's to create a situation whereby you retire at the same level of income as you enjoyed during your peak earning years. It's not going to happen by accident or by magic. It's going to happen because you make it happen through a simple

"I'M TOO BUSY RIGHT NOW"

but deliberate long term plan. It's going to happen over a period of time because you have not only learned what needs to be done — you have done what needs to be done.

INVESTMENT BEHAVIOURS OF THE RICH

Over the last several years, considerable research has been conducted on the topic of the attitudes and behaviour of affluent investors, both in Canada and the U.S. In the U.S., the Securities Industry Association has conducted annual research on the topic since the late 1980s. U.S. Trust conducted a survey of the most affluent 1% of Americans in late 1992.

In Canada, Decima Research conducted a poll on behalf of Royal Trust to examine the priorities and attitudes of the most affluent 25% of the population in the fall of 1994, and at the same time NCE Resources commissioned Dun and Bradstreet along with J. White and Associates to examine the most affluent 1% of Canadians.

Fascinating patterns emerge from the data gathered on a broad range of issues from their attitudes towards money, their view of the future, their concerns over rising taxes, the state of government pensions, their investment habits, and their attitude towards estate planning.

Below, we identify six specific behaviours which seem to distinguish the rich from the rest. This is done in the belief that we can often learn from others by simply watching and noting what they do — and then copying their behaviour. As investors try to learn from the investing greats such as Sir John Templeton, Warren Buffett, Bob Krembil and others, so can we as Canadians learn to be financially successful from those who have already done so. Here's what they do:

1. THEY USE STRATEGIC ASSET ALLOCATION TO CREATE A WELL BALANCED PORTFOLIO

These folks know that a Nobel Prize was awarded in 1990 to Dr. William F. Sharpe of Stanford University and Dr. Harry M. Markowitz of the University of Chicago, for studies carried out over the previous several decades which led to break-through research confirming that we can **increase returns and reduce risk** through the use of Strategic Asset Allocation. This research proved academically what many know intuitively: it's best not to put all your eggs in one basket.

And so they are diversified both geographically and by asset class. They are much more likely for example to invest internationally than middle class Canadians; 65% of the rich do it as compared to only 31% of the middle class. They are also much more likely to use a broad range of asset categories which include real estate, inflation hedges like gold, oil and gas, and both Canadian and international equities rather than limiting themselves, as others are more inclined to, to cash and fixed income investments.

They use a balanced portfolio, because they know from Sharpe & Markowitz' research (subsequently reinforced and validated by numerous other scientific studies) that 80% to 90% of a portfolio's return comes as a result of the mix or balance of assets within it; this asset allocation decision is the **single most important investment decision we make**. They have learned that such considerations as market timing and different management styles are of comparatively minor significance. They also know that the choice of individual security (be it stock, bond or mutual fund) is among the least significant factors . . . despite the fact that this is the decision **most** people spend **most** time on. They therefore construct a balanced portfolio . . . and let it work for them.

2. THEY BELIEVE IN AND USE EQUITIES

Over and over again, research from all over the world demonstrates clearly that over the longer term, equities outperform other asset categories — specifically the fixed income alternative with which Canadians have historically been fixated.

The most affluent understand that equities represent the "engine" or the "locomotive" of an investment portfolio, and that equities are an absolutely necessary component to ensure results which will vault our returns ahead of taxes and inflation.

They understand too that equities are more favourably taxed than fixed income vehicles.

And so we find that nearly 60% of Canada's rich have 40% or more of their portfolios in equities, as compared to the middle class where only about 16% of investors have that much in equities.

Could it possibly be that an **understanding** of the value of equities, combined with actually **using** them in a portfolio, helps to make the rich rich? Absolutely!

3. THEY USE MUTUAL FUNDS

The rich know the value of hiring professionals to assist them in achieving their goals. The use of mutual funds for them is a logical extension of this understanding. They often don't have the time, the inclination, maybe even the expertise to identify the specific components of their investment portfolio. And so nearly 75% of the rich use mutual funds compared to between 30% and 40% of the rest of the population.

4. THEY USE TAX SHELTER OPPORTUNITIES

The best tax shelter available to Canadians (next to their home) is the RRSP, and the rich take full advantage of the opportunity. Virtually all of them make the full contribution allowed!

Compare that to the rest of Canadians where in 1995 only about 25% of us contributed less than 20% of the amount for which we were eligible.

It's true that beyond their RRSPs, the rich like the rest of Canadians, do not make as much use of other tax shelter opportunities including mutual fund limited partnerships, oil and gas funds, and others as they might. Much of this is attributed to the fact that they just don't **know** very much about these options yet. The rich do however seem to be more receptive to tax shelter opportunities than the population at large.

5. THEY HAVE AN ESTATE PLAN IN PLACE

Nearly 90% of the rich have an estate plan, including a current will, in place as compared to only about 40% of the middle class.

They seem to understand the dangers of dying without a will ("intestate") which include the fact that their assets may well be distributed by a public official in a way quite contrary to their wishes. . . and they've taken steps to prevent that from happening.

As part of their estate plan, they are also likely to have taken steps to reduce the amount of probate fees payable (these fees have been **tripled** in Ontario over the last few years), and to have in place a Continuing Power of Attorney which will allow for a smooth administration of their assets in the event of their mental and/or physical incapacity.

An estate plan is necessary for **everyone** who has assets to pass along, regardless of the size of the assets or your age.

It seems from these statistics that the rich are not only more determined to grow their assets; they are also more determined to preserve them.

6. THEY USE FINANCIAL ADVISORS

According to the NCE study, the rich are 3 1/2 times more likely to use the services of a financial advisor than the rest of the population. Many of those interviewed stated categorically that the advice they received prompted them to do the very things that assisted them to become wealthy: to develop a balanced portfolio, to include equities in their portfolio, to use mutual funds, to use tax shelter opportunities, and to develop a comprehensive estate plan.

In fact, a groundbreaking study conducted in the U.S. from January 1983 to September 1993 asked the question: "Do the services of an independent financial planner make a difference?" The results were conclusive. U.S. mutual fund investors who purchased mutual funds through an independent advisor did nearly 20% better than those who purchased no load funds on their own.

Similar results were found in a similar study conducted in Canada. Interviews were conducted with 1,890 Canadians to determine their financial performance over the three-year period between 1989 and 1992. Those who utilized the services of an independent financial advisor realized net asset growth that was 34% higher than the financial returns achieved by investors who made their own financial decisions, and did not receive outside professional advice during that three-year time period.

Since this period was one of the most volatile in modern investment history, these results would not be surprising. The superior, professionally advised returns on invested capital was most often achieved by following advice to move assets out of real estate and fixed income securities into bond funds, international equities, and domestic mutual funds as well as learning to anticipate the interest rate cycle.

Furthermore, 90% of the rich update their financial plan annually or more than once a year. They understand the Chinese proverb which states, "If you don't know where you're going, any road will do." These people have a very clear idea of where they are going and they are receiving assistance to get there.

Only 10% of the rest of the population makes use of the services of a financial advisor, which may help to account for the fact that this huge majority of Canadians are simply not, on a consistent basis, taking some of the relatively few but immensely important actions that can literally make them rich, at least in a financial sense.

CONCLUSION

It's not necessary to reinvent the wheel. We can learn by watching and imitating successful people in almost every walk of life from sports, to business, to entertainment, to finance.

If the rich are more financially successful because they use a balanced portfolio approach with a significant position in equities, because they have retirement and estate plans, because they use the services of investment managers and financial advisors, and because they use key tax reduction opportunities, then perhaps, just perhaps . . . middle income Canadians could follow a similar plan to achieve improved investment results with higher returns, lower risk, and greater financial security. It seems like a reasonable assumption.

The six behaviours described here are not difficult to apply. It simply takes a decision to do so and the persistence to stick with it.

Coach's Quote

If you can dream it, you can do it! Do it right and do it now!

Remember, there are three types of people in the world. Some people make things happen; some people watch things happen; and some say "What happened?" The rich get rich by **making** things happen . . . and you can too.

· POST-GAME RECAP ·

How to Achieve Financial Independence

1. Pay yourself first
2. Invest consistently and over the long term (time and consistency)
3. Maximize your RRSP contribution every year using dollar cost averaging
4. Become an owner, not a loaner
5. Invest in solidly performing, well managed mutual funds
6. Learn and apply the magic of compounding
7. Learn and use the Rule of 72 to enable your money to double as quickly as possible
8. Pay off your mortgage
9. Buy low-cost term insurance only
10. Pay your credit cards off monthly
11. Use all the tax saving options at your disposal

FINDING A MONEY COACH

You are forced to play the "money game" from the time you begin to earn a living until you die, and many of us will play it for 40, 50, 60 years or more. Don't you agree that when you're going to play a game for that length of time, it makes sense to be able to play it as well as possible? There are rules to the game and there are strategies you can use to play more effectively and successfully.

In this game, it's important to know who your teammates are and who's the "opposition." Revenue Canada makes the rules, interprets the rules, and enforces the rules of the game — Revenue Canada is not on your "team."

To learn the rules and strategies of the money game, you need a "money coach" to work with you over the long term, and more and more people are coming to this conclusion.

If, like many others, you are too busy to take the time to learn all the rules and strategies, or if you don't have the interest, the ability or the inclination to learn them, then you need to find expert advice.

It's true that books like this one can provide some useful assistance, but your personal situation is unlikely to be covered in any book. You really need an individual to coach you over the long term, in all aspects of your financial life. It's my sincere belief that an experienced professional advisor can help you save thousands of dollars in taxes over time, and can increase the value of your portfolio over what you can do yourself by many thousands of dollars.

Why would you not use the expertise of someone who can help you achieve those results? Well, more and more people are recognizing the advantages of seeking a "money coach!" But where do you look to find one?

Some people use a bank manager, but their expertise generally is limited to loans or mortgages. Accountants are often thought to be good money coaches and no doubt many are. Again we'd suggest you look for someone with a broader overview. Tax considerations are significant, but there are many others that need to be taken into account in creating an overall financial strategy. Lawyers are often relied upon for general financial and investment advice, but they are not trained in investment theory and may have no expertise in the area of asset allocation or in personal taxation.

I recommend you seek out someone whose professional career is completely focused on providing expert, pertinent, and timely financial advice.

WHAT QUALIFICATIONS SHOULD YOUR MONEY COACH HOLD?

Generally, someone in the field will have at least completed the Investment Funds course which (along with being registered by the appropriate Securities Commission) allows one to sell mutual funds to the public. The Canadian Securities Course (along with the appropriate registration) allows one to sell a full range of securities (including stocks and bonds as well as mutual funds). Stockbrokers have all completed the Canadian Securities Course.

But those are minimum qualifications — both prerequisites for anyone registered to sell securities. You should also look for an advisor who has completed (or is enrolled in) the Certified Financial Planner (CFP) or the Registered Financial Planner (RFP) designation. The CFP is offered by the Canadian Securities Institute as part of their ongoing educational programs. The RFP is offered by the Canadian Association of Financial Planners. Both cover many pertinent topics such as taxation, personal financial planning, asset management, estate planning, etc.

Some people take advanced programs offered by the Canadian Securities Institute and include the FCSI designation (Fellow of the Canadian Securities Institute) or the new Canadian Investment Manager (CIM) designation.

Any of these programs ensure that your advisor has a commitment to ongoing professional development which will likely be beneficial to you.

As well, you should probably expect that your advisor would be a member of the Canadian Institute of Financial Planners and adhere to its Code of Ethics.

HOW DO YOU FIND THE RIGHT ADVISOR?

Many advisors provide an ongoing series of educational seminars which are intended to provide up-to-the-moment information on trends in the economy, which funds are "hot", methods of tax reduction, and so on. You may find it worthwhile to attend some of these and get a sense of whether you could work with that individual.

Following are some questions you can ask that will help you to decide upon the "money coach" who's right for you.

1. What type of licensing do you hold? What type of products is your company licensed to sell *(i.e., mutual funds, insurance, full securities)?*

2. What is your education? How much experience do you have in the business? What credentials do you hold in the business?

3. How often will you contact me? Will I meet with you or a junior assistant? How much administrative support do you have?

4. Do you prepare a comprehensive proposal addressing my overall financial situation? What type of progress report will you provide? How often?

5. How are you paid? Are you reimbursed by the financial institutions whose products you sell? Do you charge a flat fee? A percentage of the value of the portfolio? A combination? What choices do I have?

6. What types of clients do you deal with mostly? Will you give me references?

7. Why should I work with you rather than someone else? What sets you apart from other advisors?

An individual who can respond effectively and comprehensively to this barrage of questions is probably someone who can provide real value to you, your portfolio, and your entire financial situation.

Ask tough questions before you hire a coach!

• COACH'S PLAYBOOK •

How to choose your own money coach

If the services of a money coach are to be used to maximum advantage, it's important to select that coach wisely. Like any professional relationship, it will flourish if both parties remain comfortable in it, if there is trust and mutual respect, and if your confidence in the coach remains at a high level.

How then can you decide on who you will work with? The following guidelines can help.

1. Ask friends for referrals.

If a friend whose judgement and advice you trust can offer a referral based on his or her experience, you're probably going to be happy too.

2. Ask for the names of two or three current clients.

Call these people and ask them questions about their experience with this coach. Ask whether they would recommend him or her to their friends. Ask them what they like best about their coach, and finish by asking them what they like least about him or her. Their answer to that last question will tell you all you need to know.

3. Ask to see a few sample financial plans.

A reasonable plan should include information describing the current financial picture, an indication of desired future results that can be measured (complete with timelines), and a series of recommendations directly related to the desired future results. While many plans tend to go on for pages, I prefer them to be "one page simple."

4. Choose an independent.

Some coaches are actually sales representatives for a single insurance company or group of mutual funds and can sell that insurance or those mutual funds only. Understandably, they will represent their product as being "all you'll ever need."

The fact is, however, that some mutual funds have performed better than others over the years and that some insurance companies offer lower rates than others. There are simply too many good products and companies out there to allow yourself to be restricted to the use of only one.

Work with an "independent" who represents a wide range of companies and products, and who will "shop the market" for you to offer the best products available. Within reason, I believe that a wider choice is better than a narrow choice.

5. Ask what range of services they provide.

The wider the range of services they provide, the easier it will be for you. Can they offer mutual funds, insurance, mortgage-backed securities, GICs, RRSPs, RRIFs, and annuities? Do they offer a mortgage-arranging service? Do they do income tax returns? Do they provide you with ongoing information updates through the use of a regular newsletter? Do they offer occasional large group presentations for their clients to be kept informed of changing tax laws, economic conditions, etc.?

Taken together, these guidelines can help you choose the coach who's right for you.

A GLOSSARY OF TERMS

Administrator: The person appointed by the court to administer the estate when there is no will, the will did not name an Executor or the named Executor has died or is unwilling to act. Also referred to as a "personal representative".

Agent For Executor: Where a trust company is hired by the named Executor for a fee to provide advice and administration services.

Alternate Appointment: An alternative Executor appointed if the first named Executor cannot or will not act.

Amortization: The process of gradually reducing a future obligation or capital outlay with a series of payments over a pre-determined period.

Annuity: An agreement under which assets are turned over to an institution on the condition that the donor (or other designated person) receive regular payments for a specified period. Most often used as a retirement vehicle to provide the annuitant with a guaranteed income. Life annuities pay for the lifetime of the annuitant and fixed-term annuities until the annuitant reaches age 90.

Asset allocation: The relative proportions of equities, bonds, cash, real estate and other asset types held in a portfolio at a given time. In a mutual fund, the portfolio manager often varies these proportions in order to maximize return when economic conditions change.

Automatic reinvestment: An option available to investors in mutual fund or other investment whereby income (dividends, interest, or capital gains) distributions paid are used to purchase additional units of the fund.

Balanced portfolio: A balanced portfolio is the distribution of investments into several asset categories to help increase returns and reduce risk. The basic components of a balanced portfolio are cash, bonds, Canadian and international equities, real estate, oil, gas and gold. The weighting of the different components varies depending on age and one's aggressiveness as an investor.

Beneficiary: A person who receives a benefit or gift under a will, or a person for whose benefit a trust is created.

Bear market: A stock market whose index of representative stocks, such as the Toronto Stock Exchange 300 Composite Index, is declining in value. A "bearish" investor believes share prices will fall.

Blue chip stocks: Stocks with good investment qualities. They are usually common shares of well-established companies with good earning records and regular dividend payments that are known nationally for the quality and wide acceptance of their products and services.

Bond: A debt instrument issued by governments and corporations. A bond is a promise by the issuer to pay the full amount of the debt on maturity, plus interest payments at regular intervals.

Bull market: A stock market whose index has been rising in value. A "bullish" investor believes share prices will rise.

Canada Pension Plan (Quebec Pension Plan for residents of that province): Begun in 1966, CPP benefits are available to all working Canadians who have contributed to it. The amount of benefits paid depends on contributions made (most people will have paid the maximum) and your age.

Canada Deposit Insurance Corporation (CDIC): An agency of the Government of Canada which insures the deposits of Canadians in banks and trust companies up to $60,000.

Capital beneficiary: A beneficiary who is or may become entitled to the capital of the trust.

Capital gain (loss): A profit (or loss) made on the sale of an asset when the market price rises above the purchase price — usually in real estate, stocks, bonds, or other capital assets.

Certified cultural property: A gift to a designated cultural institution of property considered to have special significance by The Canadian Cultural Property Export Review Board.

Charitable gift annuity: A life annuity issued by a charitable organization for which the individual pays more than the expected annuity payments. Any capital in the account at death reverts to the issuer for use in charitable work.

Charitable remainder trust: A donation strategy in which you transfer property to a trust and name a charity as the capital beneficiary. Until then, the income beneficiary can use the property and receive any income it generates.

Codicil: An amendment to a will which makes changes or additions. It's executed with the same formalities as a will.

Common share: A class of stock that represents ownership, or equity, in a company. Common shares entitle the holder to a share in the company's profits, usually as a dividend. They may also carry a voting privilege.

Compounding: Reinvesting interest as capital to earn additional interest.

Compound interest: Interest earned on the amount invested, plus previously accumulated interest earnings. This may occur daily, weekly, monthly, quarterly, semi-annually, or annually.

Convertible term: Term life insurance which can be converted to any permanent or whole life policy without evidence of insurability, subject to time limitations.

Decreasing term: Insurance benefits reduced monthly or yearly with the premium remaining constant. (In standard policies, premiums increase and benefits remain constant.)

Deferred annuity: An annuity where payments begin after the annuity is purchased — usually after a given number of years or at certain ages.

Deferred gift: A charitable donation arranged now for payment sometime in the future, often after death.

Deferred Sales Charge (DSC): An increasingly popular alternative for mutual funds that charge front-end acquisition fees. Here, a fee is paid when the investor sells units in the fund. This usually begins at 4.5% of the units' value in the first year and declines by 0.5% to 1% per year, eventually reaching 0% several years into the future. Sometimes called an Exit Fee.

Distributions: The payments made by a mutual fund to its unit holders of the interest, dividends, and/or capital gains earned during the year. Shareholders may either take distributions in cash or reinvest them in additional shares of the fund.

Diversification: Spreading investment risk by investing in a variety of companies operating in different industries and/or countries.

Dividend: A portion of a company's profit paid out to common and preferred shareholders, the amount having been decided on by the company's board of directors. A dividend may be in the form of cash or additional stock. A preferred dividend is usually a fixed amount, while a common dividend may fluctuate with the earnings of the company.

Dollar cost averaging: An investment program in which contributions are made at regular intervals with specific and equal dollar amounts. This often results in a lower average cost per unit because more units are purchased when the prices are depressed than when they are high.

Earned income: For tax purposes, loosely defined as the total of income from employment, self-employment, pensions, and alimony. Losses from rental property and self employment may be deducted from these amounts.

Encroach (on capital): Many trust agreements provide for a named person to get the income for life, with the capital ultimately going to somebody else. The agreement may also provide the trustee(s) with the power to pay capital from the trust to a beneficiary if certain conditions for using the capital are met. The encroachment power may be limited to specific needs, such as "for education" or "in case of sickness", or very broad, such as "for the general benefit" of the beneficiary.

Endowment fund: A donation made to fund a specific purpose. The charity invests the donation and uses the income generated to fund the specified project.

Equity funds: Mutual funds that invest in common and preferred shares.

Estate: All assets owned by an individual at the time of death. The estate includes all funds, personal effects, interests in business enterprises, titles to property, real estate and chattels, and evidence of ownership, such as stocks, bonds, and mortgages owned, and notes receivable.

Estate freeze: An arrangement limiting the growth in value of the freezor's estate, by diverting the growth, usually to a subsequent generation.

Exchange privilege: The ability of a shareholder to transfer investments from one mutual fund to another within a "family" of funds managed by the same company. This exchange may or may not be accompanied by a transaction fee which is based on the asset value of the transfer.

Ex-Dividend: The date on which distributions that have been declared by a mutual fund are deducted from total net assets. The price of the fund's shares or units will be reduced by the amount of the distribution.

Executor(m)/executrix(f): The person(s) or institution named under a will to administer an estate in accordance with the terms of the will. If the will requires a trust to be established, rather than having the assets distributed outright to the beneficiaries, the Executor(trix) will normally also be named as trustee.

Fiduciary duty: The level of obligation assumed by a trustee. A fiduciary duty implies the highest level of care in dealing with property on behalf of a beneficiary.

Fixed-income funds: Mutual funds that invest in mortgages, bonds, or a combination of both. Mortgages and bonds are issued at a fixed rate of interest and are known as fixed-income securities.

Front-end commission charge: An acquisition fee based on the total value of mutual fund units purchased. The fees can range from 2% to 9%, but average 4% to 5% on most purchases.

GIC (Guaranteed Investment Certificate): A deposit certificate usually issued by a bank or trust company. An interest bearing investment that matures after a specified term, usually anywhere from 30 days to 5 years. The interest remains fixed during this period.

Gift in kind: A gift of property other than money.

Gift to the crown: A donation to a federal or provincial government body or a Crown foundation authorized to raise money for institutions such as universities, hospitals, museums, and libraries.

Grant of probate: A certificate confirming the authority set out in a will to administer a particular estate; issued to an Executor by the court. Also called Grant of Letter Probate and Letters Probate.

Guardian: The person named to be legally responsible for the minor children should both parents die.

Growth stock: Shares of a company whose earnings are expected to grow faster than average.

Guaranteed Income Supplement: A monthly payment made by the federal government to low income households. It is based on a means test and paid only to seniors with little or no income beyond Old Age Security (OAS) payments.

Guaranteed term: The length of time for which annuity payments are guaranteed. If the annuitant dies before the specified term, payments to the beneficiary will continue until the term ends.

Income: The money generated on an ongoing basis through the investment of the capital (e.g., interest and dividends).

Income beneficiary: The person or persons entitled to the income generated by the trust property until the time the trust is wound up. The income includes dividends and interest, but does not normally include capital gains, which form part of the capital. See also "life tenant".

Income splitting: The process of diverting taxable income from an individual in a high tax bracket to one in a lower tax bracket.

Index fund: A mutual fund designed to match the performance of a recognized group of publicly traded stocks, such as those represented by the TSE 300 Index or the Standard & Poor 500 Index in the U.S.

Interest: What a borrower is obliged to pay to a lender for the use of a fixed sum of money.

Inter vivos trust: Also known as a living trust, inter vivos trusts come into effect during the lifetime of the settlor.

Intestate: The legal status of someone who dies without leaving a valid will.

Investment: Using money for the purpose of obtaining income, capital gains, or both.

Intestate distribution: Where the estate left by a person who died without a will is distributed according to a predetermined formula.

Investment fund: See Mutual fund.

Irrevocable trust: A trust which cannot be revoked (cancelled) by the person who created the trust (settlor).

Issue: All persons who have descended from a common ancestor. It is a broader term than children which is limited to one generation.

Joint-and-last survivor annuity: A type of annuity that pays benefits until both annuitant and the annuitant's spouse die.

Joint tenants: A form of joint owner results in the immediate transfer of ownership to the surviving joint owner or owners.

Leverage: Using borrowed funds to maximize the rate of return on investment. A potentially dangerous strategy if the investment declines in value.

LIF (Life Income Fund): An investment option now available to people who do not wish to use locked-in RRSP funds to buy an annuity at age 69. Purchase of a LIF allows one to delay the purchase of an annuity until age 80. A LIF is eligible to use the same range of investments available in a RRIF.

Life tenant: A beneficiary who has an interest in trust property for the balance of that beneficiary's life (a life interest). For example, a trust might be set up which allows a named person to live in a house rent-free so long as he or she lives, with the house being transferred to the capital beneficiary when the life tenant dies. Or, the beneficiary may be entitled to receive all of the income from the trust investments for life.

Limited partnership: See Tax shelter.

Line of credit: A flexible type of borrowing facility that allows you to borrow up to a prescribed limit and pay interest only on the amount used.

Liquidity: The ease with which an asset can be sold and converted into cash at its full value.

Living trust: A trust created by a settlor while he or she is alive. Also referred to as an inter vivos trust.

Management fee: The amount paid annually by a mutual fund to its managers. The average annual fee in Canada is between 1% and 2% of the value of the fund's assets.

Marginal tax rate: The rate at which tax is calculated on the next dollar of income earned. This rate increases at progressively higher income brackets.

Market timing: The process of shifting from one type of investment to another with the intention of maximizing your return as market conditions change.

MBS (Mortgage backed securities): These securities provide higher yields than many other savings options by investing in first mortgages on residential properties.

Money market fund: Fixed income mutual funds that invest in short-term securities (maturing within one year).

Mortgage: A legal instrument given by a borrower to the lender entitling the lender to take over pledged property if conditions of the loan are not met.

Mutual fund: A professionally managed pool of assets, representing the contributions of many investors, which is used to purchase a portfolio of securities that meets specific investment objectives. Units are offered for sale by the fund on a continuous basis; the fund will also buy back units at their current price (net asset value per share). Sometimes called an investment fund. The most common type of fund is known as an "open end fund."

Net Asset Value Per Share (NAVPS): The total market value of all securities owned by a mutual fund, less its liabilities, divided by the number of units outstanding.

No-load fund: A mutual fund that does not charge a fee for buying or selling its units.

Old Age Security: Federal government benefits paid monthly to all Canadians at age 65, whether or not they are retired. Payments are indexed to inflation.

Personal net worth: The difference between your assets and your liabilities.

Planned giving: A charitable gift made in such a way that you maximize your tax and estate planning benefits.

Portfolio: A group of securities held or owned for investment purposes by an individual or institution. An investor's portfolio may contain common and preferred shares, bonds, options, and other types of securities.

Power of attorney: Gives signing authority for your affairs to a spouse or other trusted person in case of accident or other circumstances that leave you unable to manage your own affairs.

Present gift: A charitable donation in which the gift is made now, not at some future point.

Probate of will: Formal proof before the proper officer or court that the will offered is the last will of the testator and confirming the Executor(s) named.

Probateable assets: Those assets which pass through the estate, and which are governed by the probate document.

Prospectus: A legal document describing a new issue of securities or a mutual fund that is to be sold to the public. The prospectus must be prepared in accordance with provincial securities commission regulations. It must contain information on any material facts that can have an impact on the value of the investment—such as the fund's investment objectives and policies, services offered, or fees charged. It must also identify any investment restrictions, as well as the officers of the company.

Real rate of return: The stated rate of return, less inflation and taxes.

Renewable term: A term life insurance policy that may be renewed at prescribed rates without evidence of insurability.

RESP (Registered Education Savings Plan): A savings program for post–secondary education which earns tax-sheltered income. This income is taxable when taken out by the beneficiary of the plan, but he or she will usually have limited income when at school, and will therefore pay little tax.

Retirement gratuity: See Retiring allowance.

Retiring allowance: A lump sum paid to some employees on retirement. Usually the amount is limited to the equivalent of 50% of the final year's salary. Can be "rolled" into an RRSP.

Reverse mortgage: A means of borrowing that allows a retired homeowner to use the equity built up in a home to receive a lump sum of cash, as well as monthly tax-free income through the purchase of an annuity.

Revocable Trust: A trust that gives the settlor the power to revoke the trust.

Risk: The possibility that some or all of the money put into an investment will be lost.

Risk-free return: The return available from securities that have no risk of loss. Short term securities issued by the government (such as Treasury Bills) normally provide a risk-free return.

Risk tolerance: The ability of a person to tolerate risk. Risk tolerance is a function of the individual's personality and other factors, and is an important element in determining investment strategy.

RRIF (Registered Retirement Income Fund): A non-annuity investment vehicle for maturing RRSPs. One of the options available to RRSP holders upon cashing in their retirement funds at age 69 or sooner. RRIFs generally provide for a series of payments which increase each year.

RRSP (Registered Retirement Savings Plan): A savings program approved by Revenue Canada that permits tax-deferred saving for retirement purposes. Contributions to an RRSP are tax deductible. Earnings on contributions are sheltered from tax while they remain in the plan.

Rule of 72: A simple mathematical calculation used to determine how quickly money doubles in value. In order to determine the number of years required, divide 72 by the rate of return.

Self-directed RRSP: An RRSP whose investments are controlled by the plan holder. A self-directed RRSP may include stocks, bonds, residential mortgages, or other types of investments approved by Revenue Canada.

Settlement: The transfer of property to a trust.

Settlor: The individual who established a trust.

Spousal RRSP contribution: A contribution by a taxpayer to an RRSP held by his or her spouse. The amount is counted against the contributor's yearly RRSP limit and can be used as a tax deduction on the contributor's tax return, but remains part of the spouse's plan.

Spousal trust: A trust, as recognized under the Income Tax Act, under which the spouse is entitled to all of the income for his or her lifetime, and nobody but the spouse has a right to any of the capital while the spouse is alive. Spousal trusts are most commonly created as testamentary trusts. The major benefit of a spousal trust is that the transfer of property to the trust does not trigger a capital gain.

Tax deferral: The use of various (legal) methods to postpone the payment of income taxes until a later date.

Tax shelter: An investment that, by government regulation, can be made with untaxed or partly-taxed dollars. The creation of tax losses in order to offset an individual's taxable income from other sources thereby reduces tax liability.

Taxable income: The amount of your annual income that is used to calculate how much income tax must be paid; your total earnings for the year, minus deductions.

Term deposit: Similar to a guaranteed investment certificate. An interest-bearing investment to which an investor commits funds for a specified term and rate of interest.

Tenants-in-common: A form of joint ownership in which two or more persons own the same property in equal or differing proportions. At the death of a tenant-in-common, ownership of the deceased's share transfers to that person's estate, not to the other joint owner.

Term insurance: A form of life insurance designed to provide coverage over a specific period.

Testamentary trust: A trust set up in a will that only takes effect after death.

Testate: A person who dies having left a valid will.

Testator/testatrix: The individual who makes a will.

Trust: A legal arrangement in which one person (the settlor) transfers legal title to a trustee (a fiduciary) to manage the property for the benefit of a person or institution (the beneficiaries).

Trustee: The person or trust company that manages property according to the instructions in the trust agreement and laws governing trustees.

Total return: The amount of income earned from an investment, together with its capital appreciation, expressed as a percentage of the original amount invested. It indicates an investment's performance over a stated period.

Treasury Bills: Short-term debt securities sold by governments, usually with maturities of three months to one year. They carry no stated interest rate, but trade at a discount to their face value. The discount represents the return.

Unit: In mutual funds, a unit represents a portion, or share, of the total value of the fund. Units are purchased by investors, and rise or fall proportionately with the net asset value of the fund.

Universal life: A life insurance policy in which premiums are credited to an account from which periodic charges for life insurance are deducted and to which earnings are credited. Accumulated growth takes place tax free.

Whole life: Life insurance policies that provide a death benefit and cash value. The cash value is funded by premiums that are much higher than the actual cost of the coverage— particularly in the early years of the policy.

Will: A legal document, prepared by a person in compliance with formal requirements, which takes effect on his/her death and which states what he/she wants to happen to his/her property on death.